The Unlikely Priest

by J. Perry Smith

PADRE NUESTRO BOOKS

Jacksonville, Florida 32217

The Unlikely Priest

ISBN 978-0-9839669-0-6

Printed in the United States of America

Dedication

This is dedicated to Theresa who first encouraged me to write this story…. To Marifrances who made the writing possible, and to my beloved daughters, Amy Beth and Meghan Leigh.

Acknowledgments

I was so fortunate to have Robert Pohle as my mentor and editor. He believed in this book from the beginning. There are not enough words to express my heartfelt thanks. I am most grateful to Marifrances Engelhardt whose great affection for me and this story sustained my writing and made this book possible. A note of gratitude to my former wife, E. Penny Smith, whose excellent memory and library of our letters helped reconstruct events long passed. And I so appreciate Gayle Fetteringill and Sally Hanson for their patience with me in transcribing and copy editing my work so skillfully. Finally, to my proofreaders, my wife Lisa, Don Farshing, Helen Likins, and Monica MacKenzie, I am grateful for your encouragement and support throughout what can only be described as a labor of love.

Contents

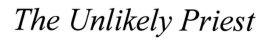

The Unlikely Priest

1 ⌗

Trick or Treat

My brother David and I approached the beautiful, castle-like mansion at the bottom of Coal Street. A turret on the front of the house gave it a foreboding look.

The richest woman in Logan County, West Virginia, lived there, and she was a recluse. She was a thin, small framed, stern-looking woman and the kids in town imagined her to be a witch. On warm days, she could sometimes be seen out in her garden. Her husband had made his money in lumbering and built this house for her years earlier. Even at our tender ages we knew that there was something strange about the house. Visitors were few and the blinds were always drawn. Yet, my brother and I had made our decision. We were going to knock on her door.

It was Halloween night, and with all the courage that a ten- and eight-year-old could muster, David and I yelled out in unison, "Trick-or-treat, trick-or-treat." Mrs. Hinchman opened the door rather quickly, feigning surprise and fright, as she looked us over very carefully. We were not well disguised as our version of the feuding Hatfields and McCoys. We were dressed in long johns, floppy hats and mascara mustaches, David holding an old whiskey jug and I an ancient, inoperable shotgun. She gave us our treats and then asked, "Are you the Smith boys?"

"Yes, we are," I replied.

She then asked which of us was the older, and I said that I was. She continued to stare at us, and then her eyes fell on me.

"Well then, you are the adopted one," she said.

"No, ma'am," I replied. "I am John Perry, the son of Yuma and John Smith."

"Are you the older?" she persisted.

"Yes, ma'am," came my now nervous reply.

She said, "Then you are the adopted one. Go home and ask your mother, and she will tell you."

We left her house and continued on our trick-or-treating around the neighborhood. I was shaken and scared by Mrs. Hinchman's insistence that I was adopted, but I remained quiet. Soon I grew impatient with our rounds and I wanted to get home to ask Mother if it was true.

As we were going through our candies on the kitchen table, I told my mother that Mrs. Hinchman said I was adopted. I asked her if it was true. Mother replied that Mrs. Hinchman was an old, evil woman and didn't know what she was talking about, and I should forget what she had said.

David and I were soon sent to bed, but sometime during the night I was awakened by voices in the parlor. Careful not to step on the squeaky planks along the long hall, I snuck through the house and stood outside the parlor, peering through the cracked door and straining to hear the whispered conversation. The bare hardwood floor was cold on my feet and when I heard what was being said, the cold shot through my body, piercing my heart.

All of the adult members of our extended family were sitting around the room, with the fireplace blazing, discussing how I should be told I was adopted. Mother was standing in the center of the room distraught and crying, repeatedly drying her eyes with a small flowered handkerchief. I had never seen my mother, normally a reserved, almost stoic woman, sob like this. I became completely chilled and afraid. Trembling, I went back to my bedroom, climbed into bed and cried myself to sleep.

The next morning Mother sat down next to me at the breakfast table and stiffly told me that Mrs. Hinchman had not lied. Once she got past that part, her voice softened as she told me I had indeed been adopted. Mother said that she and my father had been married sixteen years and had wanted desperately to have a baby. When no child was born to them, they made the decision to adopt. They went to an orphanage in Knoxville, Tennessee, where they were interviewed and invited to see the children who had been left there. She said the babies were in baskets. They stopped and took a long look at me because I smiled at them - the only child to do so, she explained. She said that, because I seemed such a happy baby, they chose me.

Mother gave no details about the orphanage or why I had been placed there except that I was just a few months old. She claimed not to know anything about my biological family or where they came from. She said the orphanage did not share that kind of information with her and my father. I asked if David was also adopted.

She said, "No. I was surprised a year after we brought you

home to find I was carrying David," explaining that it was a fairly common occurrence. I asked why they had gone to Knoxville since they were living in Kentucky. "There were no orphanages in Danville or Somerset, Kentucky."

Mother dismissed further questions, and simply said, "I am your mother, I love you more than anything in the world. You are special because you came to us at a time when we believed we could not have a child. You are especially loved because we chose you as our son. Unlike many children, you were wanted. Your father and I very much wanted you to be our son." Her tone became reassuring, "You are our son, just as David is our son. You came to us in a different way. It does not mean we love you any less or differently." I believed her.

It was a tearful and scary conversation, but I knew from her embrace and the tenderness of her voice she truly loved me and I somehow sensed that she was protecting me. I also knew she was not telling me the entire truth. The story she told sounded vaguely familiar, and it was only a short while later that I recognized that I was like Moses found in the basket in the bulrushes. The similarities between Moses floating in the bulrushes and being picked out of the water were too coincidental, the language almost the same. Abandoned and then found. Found to be and become somebody special.

Even at ten years old, the odd feeling of not knowing the true story left me with a lot of questions and a twinge of shame. Precisely because of my mother's vagueness and reticence, I felt there was something shameful about my adoption. I was unnerved by my mother's story and how guarded she was about how I had come to them. I was also certain that the circumstances of my adoption would remain her secret forever, but I would not let it rest. My questions were unending. I understood clearly my birth mother had abandoned me, but I wanted to know why. I was determined to find out.

Soon I began to ask other family members, particularly my mother's sisters, Alma and Hope, how I came to be adopted. They retold Mother's version of the story. Soon I began searching the house and rummaging through my mother's personal papers and files, attempting to find clues about my adoption. I thought she might have saved the legal papers. They were nowhere to be found.

Some years later, my Aunt Alma, my favorite aunt, told me that the night the family gathered to decide what to tell me about my adoption Mother had thrown all the papers into the fireplace. The only document she saved was my new birth certificate that said I was the son of John Milton Smith and Yuma Frances Perry Smith, born on October 21, 1944, in Knoxville, Tennessee. As it turns out, when a state issues a new birth certificate in an adoption, the two pieces of information that must be true and accurate are the date and place of birth. This information would be of critical help much later in the search for my biological parents.

My mother, Yuma Smith, and I, circa. February 16, 1946
celebrating my adoption.

2 ⊞

Dancing with Fireflies

Mother loved to tell stories about her life with our father, John. He was a locomotive engineer on the Southern Railway system and had the run between Danville, Kentucky, and Chattanooga, Tennessee, for years. She said that from the first days I came to them, it became her habit to go to the train station in Danville and wait for him to pull his locomotive into the station at the end of his run. I would be in tow and my father would bring the train into the terminal area. He would come down from the engine cab to greet us and wait for the off loading of passengers or the uncoupling of coal and boxcars.

On just such a day in the spring of 1948, Mother and I were at the station and we greeted my father as we normally did. He hugged us and told Mother he would meet us at our car after he had taken the engine to the roundhouse. He climbed back aboard the diesel and told the fireman to move the engine on down the track toward the roundhouse. My father moved his heavy tool box from the back of the engine cab to the door behind his seat. When he stood up to take his seat, he fell to the floor and died.

He was 46 years old and had suffered a massive coronary. I was four years old.

My father, in death as in life, seemed larger than life. Apparently, he had a great sense of humor. He always had a joke to amuse friends and loved to sing and dance. He loved telling and hearing stories, particularly about railroading. Years after his death, I spoke to the fireman who was with him when he died. He described my father as a man "who knew no strangers."

The most remarkable statement I have heard about my father was "I have never met the person who knew your father and did not like him." That statement became ingrained in my understanding of what it was to be successful, liked and loved.

I remember how devastating it was for me the first time a man told me he did not like me. I had always known there were people who did not like me. However, to have a coworker say directly to me "I do not like you" was one of the most horrible moments of my life. This first spoken rejection was linked to the standard I had adopted based on the statement of my father's friend. I was shaken to the core and it took some time for me to get over it.

I vaguely recall my father's funeral. It was an open casket affair in our Danville home. I have photographs of his four brothers talking with one another just before the burial. I surmise it was a very sad affair. And from the pictures and the stories told, I know it was one of the most significant events of my life because it left me without a father for the rest of my life. It has taken me years to fully understand and appreciate the implications of having grown up without a father.

There were frequent stories about my father and his antics. A photograph taken in the Great Smoky Mountains shows him dancing with a bear. He looked like an Appalachian "Zorba the Greek," arms up reaching toward the sky and the bear on its hind legs appearing to imitate my father's antics or vice versa. My terrified mother took the photograph from inside a car. In the background a sign says "Danger! Do not feed or approach the bears." It was always said that my father could not resist the temptation to "cut up" and have fun.

A famous photograph of my father can still be found occasionally in government buildings. It shows the first diesel locomotive crossing the bridge trestle at Burnside, Kentucky. He is leaning out of the cab smiling and waving to the camera. He was the consummate railroader, famous on the Southern system for his humor, knowledge and experience. I think it extremely ironic that my father's family home and farm, a portion of which can be seen in the picture, is now under the waters of Lake Burnside.

My father was an exceptional railroader and good instructor who was a Road Foreman of Engines. He was the engineer who drove the last steam locomotive and the first diesel on the Southern system in the late 1940s. Mother often told the story of how proud he was to have been so honored.

One of the immediate results of my father's death was that Mother, David and I moved to her hometown in Logan, West Virginia. There we lived in a large rambling house on upper Coal Street with my grandmother and our extended family. Mother's two younger sisters, Alma and Hope, were still single and helped take care of us. Mother resumed teaching elementary school to provide for us. David and I were loved and nurtured by our grandmother, Mattie Whitman Perry, and several aunts on the Perry side of the family who lived nearby.

My early childhood was happy. It was filled with adventure in the mountains that surrounded our home. Native American history and lore in the persons of Mingo Chief Logan, and Princess Aracoma, daughter of Shawnee Chief Cornstalk, and "playin' cowboys and Indians" filled our imaginations.

One summer day I was on the side of the hill in front of our house, where I caught a small green snake. I went into the kitchen looking for my grandmother to show her my prize. She was sitting in her wheelchair by the sink doing the dishes. Cupped in my hands so that it could not escape was a beautiful baby green snake.

I opened my hands to show my grandmother what I had captured and, to my horror, she let out this awful screech, pushed away from me, and overturned her wheelchair, falling onto the floor. I dropped the snake and went screaming out of the house to find my aunt to help. Aunt India came running down from her upstairs apartment. She immediately righted Grandma, getting her back into her wheelchair.

This incident caused me to be put in school that next fall. Grandma was in her late 70s and was a diabetic amputee. She refused to baby sit me any longer, deeming me an "incorrigible boy." It was always said that Grandma "didn't much care for boys since she had only raised girls" and that her marriage to Grandpa Ira had been hard since "he drank a lot," and worked only occasionally as a wallpaper hanger.

Grandma Perry had for many years run a boarding house and "taken in washin' and ironin'" to keep the family together. Life had been hard. Grandma did have a special place in her heart for my brother David, though. In retrospect, her love for David may have been because he was born to Yuma, rather than having been adopted.

Mother was teaching school at the Dehue Elementary School and she arranged for me to sit in on the first grade class, even though I was to turn five that October. Miss Jeffries was a wonderful teacher and welcomed me as though I were a regular student. The first year inoculations were the worst part of being at school. The convenience of this arrangement was that Mother and I went to school together and came home together. I was well supervised and participated in the first grade as if I belonged there. At the end of the school year, Miss Jeffries recommended that I move on to the second grade because "he has done as well as the other students."

True to mountain tradition, the older men of the family taught us to hunt and fish. Rabbit, squirrel, deer and catfish were seasonally in our meals. My least favorite meal was squirrel gravy with eggs and biscuits for breakfast.

Another significant consequence of my father's death was that we were not well off financially. Even though I never had a sense of being poor, from a very early age I understood that I would always have to work to help support our small family. I delivered the local newspaper, *The Logan Banner*, and sold *Grit*, a popular weekly newspaper that I received by mail and then sold on the street.

Mother made "rick-rack" earrings, by gluing a stiff, colored cloth to an earring backing in a flower-like shape. They were popular with some of the older ladies, but sales fell off when they tired of my visits. I also peddled mail-order salve to "cure" all manner of the body's aches and pains. My earnings went to Mother who would then incorporate them into our budget. She allowed me to keep a nickel or dime for candy or some treat or savings.

It was during this time Mother began to introduce me as "the little man of the house." I took some pride in that new introduction because it gave me a sense of who I was or who I was becoming. The implication of being a responsible young man made me feel good. Sometimes, however, it embarrassed me. Other times I was angry that I could not play with friends because I had to work.

At about age nine, I opened my first Christmas Savings Club account at the Bank of Logan. It was almost a ceremonial event engineered by my mother who took me directly to the bank president. He seriously explained the rules for the deposits I was to make of the quarters I saved in a paper holder. Mother made quite a fuss and told almost everyone in the bank how proud she was of me. I remember being slightly embarrassed, but also feeling a sense of power and growth into a new phase of my life.

Miss Carter was a teller at the bank. She was about 20 years old, very pretty and smelled of sweet perfume. Each time I came into the bank, she invited me to her teller position. Miss Carter talked in a sweet and gentle way, letting me know she liked me. She clearly understood that I liked her because I could not stop smiling at her and finding every excuse I could to be in the bank.

I liked the way those encounters felt. Others noticed and soon my uncle and my mother teased that I was "sweet" on Miss Carter. I remember retreating ever so slightly and never wanting to be accompanied again to the bank. I didn't want to share with anyone nor did I want anyone to know how I felt about this lovely woman who was kind and smelled of lavender.

Mother was well known in Logan County as a formidable teacher and strong woman. She was almost humorless and certainly was always earnest about her profession as a teacher and her life with David and me. She had an air of formality and rectitude.

Mother was rigid in matters of education and religion. I was always surprised how strident and critical her feelings and words were with respect to the Roman Catholic Church. There was always judgment in her voice when she talked about the "idol worshipers and papists." There were no compromises about education and religion.

Yet, I learned, as I became more educated, that there were huge gaps in her education about religion, science, anthropology and history in general. It was, for example, impossible to talk to her about Darwin's theory of evolution. "God created Man!" she would declare and that was that! "There were no apes involved with God's work."

These years in Logan were wonderful years of discovery and exciting times with my brother and friends. We caught snakes and frogs. We built dams in a creek bed, collected tadpoles and danced away the summer nights with "light'n bugs." We would illuminate ball jars, collecting as many as we could. The unfortunate light'n bugs were those who were sacrificed to make rings on our fingers.

We built bonfires for potato and corn roasts. There were marshmallows and watermelons. Family gatherings always involved food and storytelling, remembrance and song. Somehow there was always a musician in our midst, a banjo picker, a guitar to be strummed or a piano to be played.

Our family was large - aunts, uncles and cousins with names like Perry, Whitman, Ellis, Johnson, Hatfield and Mitchell. It was a puzzle who was a second, third or fourth cousin, but it was important to know that stuff because it was about who you were and from whence you came. Life was about being connected to the clan. We were descendants of "Scotch-Irish," or "Black-Irish," or German and English immigrants. Our Appalachian speech patterns, idioms and music were expressions of our dominant Celtic heritage. Everyone I have ever met from West Virginia was somehow connected to either the Hatfields or the McCoys, the famous fight'n hillbillies, and we were no exception. We were related to both of the famous feuding clans.

Dehue Elementary was in a company-owned coal mining camp and was dirty with soot and dust in the classrooms and on the playground. Jumping rope, playing Ring-around-the-Rosie, "shoot'n marbles" and romping on the jungle gym held our attention during every recess, a dirty affair that required a bath every night. At bath time my mother would often rhetorically ask, "John Perry, how do you get so dirty?"

I loved fall and winter days because I liked the smell of the burning coal stoves in our buildings, and if you were well behaved the teacher might let you throw coal into the small pot-bellied stoves that warmed our annex buildings.

At Dehue Elementary I experienced the first violence of my life. An older student enticed me to box him and he promptly bloodied my nose. "Seein'stars" was not my idea of fun. Not long after, I saw real violence on the school grounds.

One spring afternoon a young man, in his late teens, wandered onto the school grounds during recess and began menacing all of us there with a crow bar. He eventually hit the principal with the crow bar, knocking him to the ground. I got a sick feeling from the thud of the impact and seeing the principal fall to the ground. Horrified, we all ran into our classrooms. Sheriff's deputies came and finally arrested the boy down by the riverbank where he was hiding. It is my first recollection of being really afraid.

Shortly after discovering I was adopted, Mother started dating a man, Owen, she desperately wanted David and me to accept. He was a coal miner, a crude and vulgar sort. No one in our family liked him or understood Mother's attraction or interest in him. She would tell us we needed a father, and when we protested, she would drop using the term father and say, "Well, it would be good for us to have a man around the house."

One late spring afternoon, on a payday Friday, Owen came to our house roaring drunk. He cursed and yelled for what seemed a very long time. It was a loud scene with my aunts and Mother trying to get him to leave our home. When I tried to stand up for my mother, Owen grabbed a large kitchen knife and began to wield it around screaming, "I'll cut your fuckin' little head off." I ran for our bedroom and got under the bed, somehow pulling David under with me.

The row continued for a time with Owen, knife still in hand, now in the street spewing obscenities and threats. David and I watched from our bedroom window. Soon the city police arrived, disarmed him easily, and put him in handcuffs. He began to cry, hanging his head, slobbering and throwing up, begging not to be taken to jail. He disgusted me and I saw he was a coward and a "mean drunk" as some called it. My face was pressed against the windowpane, straining to see and hear all that was said.

As the police "paddy wagon" drove away, I promised myself I would never again allow myself to be so terrified and caught unprepared to defend myself. Soon after, I began to fantasize about becoming a policeman or deputy sheriff.

My father, John M. Smith, circa. 1943

3 ⌗

Catholic Beginnings

Almost immediately after learning I was adopted, my imagination began to run wild with possible scenarios as to how my adoption really occurred. I never, even at the age of ten, believed Mother's Moses story. It just did not ring true. Mother's reticence about the adoption only intensified my curiosity.

For some strange reason, and perhaps because some of my favorite schoolmates were Roman Catholic and ethnic Italians, I began to gravitate toward their families and religion. My afternoon paper route took me by Our Lady of Mt. Carmel Roman Catholic Church. There was a young priest, Father Hickey, there and a number of nuns who taught catechism classes.

I created the story that I was adopted from a Roman Catholic orphanage. This made absolutely no sense since my family was protestant and had long belonged to the First Christian Church (Disciples of Christ) in Logan. However, it was the story I chose and it pleased me. I suppose, in some distorted way, it made me feel I was different. It made me stand out in the sense that it wasn't just any orphanage; it was a Roman Catholic orphanage.

One rainy, dreary fall afternoon, I screwed up my courage to visit Father Hickey in his rectory behind the church. I had frequently attended mass with my friend John Riggio for some months, so I had some sense of the order of things at Mt. Carmel. I told Father Hickey my amazing story about the staunch protestant woman, Yuma Smith, who adopted me from a Roman Catholic orphanage. Even more incredible, Father Hickey asked for scant details. At the end of my story, he told me that he had seen me at mass and wondered about me. He asked why I came to see him and I told him I wanted to become a Roman Catholic.

I had no idea where that notion came from, except that I liked the ceremony, ritual and mystery of the mass. What I did not say was that I also liked my friends who were Roman Catholic and I wanted to be like them because they were different from my family and our usual circle of friends. They had what I thought was real identity where I had none. Somehow, I had now begun to think of myself as an orphan. I was no longer who I had thought I was, therefore I could become who I wanted.

Father Hickey said he could not baptize me as a Roman Catholic without the proper preparation. More important, however, he said, "I cannot baptize you without permission from your mother." My heart sank, knowing full well she would never give her permission. She had already expressed considerable dismay about my interest in the Roman Catholic Church, and had asked our pastor, A.J. Coffey, to intervene.

Pastor Coffey tried to talk to me several times when I accompanied Mother to church, but I was very much put off by his cold demeanor and certainty about how he thought the Catholic Church was hell bound. I was repulsed by the name-calling, "idol worshipers, blood drinkers, nun fornicators," and other characterizations, which made no sense, based on my experience with my friends, Father Hickey and the nuns that I had come to know. They were always kind, understanding, polite, proper and respectful. Perhaps more important, they welcomed me and I felt at home.

Father Hickey, without explanation, decided to begin my instruction in the Catholic faith. He gave me a Miraculous Medal, which he took from his own neck. He also gave me a copy of The Baltimore Catechism to read and study. He encouraged me to memorize the Our Father, the Hail Mary and the Glory Be. At a later time, Father Hickey taught me to say the Rosary. That ritual was perfected under the instruction of the nuns on Wednesday afternoons, when I surreptitiously, or so I thought, attended catechism classes.

My cover story was delivering newspapers. I thought I was clever and my mother would never learn that I was taking an hour out to attend catechism classes. I was soon discovered because Pastor Coffey lived in the neighborhood and he saw me around the grounds of Mount Carmel regularly. He told my mother, who was distraught, and at the same time, puzzled. We argued about "the Catholics" as she disdainfully called them, and I was frequently punished for "sneak'n-off" to go to Mt. Carmel.

I practiced my new-found faith covertly, using every excuse and every chore I could possibly dream up to escape my mother's supervision, ending up at catechism class or mass. I would visit the nuns often, always ready to help them clean up around the property. They always seemed glad to see me and rewarded me with cookies and milk and conversation. I enjoyed their company enormously; with quiet demeanor, they were attentive and very tolerant of a ten-year-old, whom they must have understood as a "seeker," just as they were. It was not a point I would have understood clearly at that time, but I always had a sense of being cared for in some way. It was comforting and energizing.

I wanted to belong to something greater than what I was or where I had come from. I wanted to be special, as special as my mother had described me in the context of the adoption. My mother frequently said that I was a special gift. I suppose I wanted to believe that in every possible way. Therefore, beginning at a very young age I tried to be special, different, to stand out in some way.

It was odd that I chose to become a Roman Catholic even though I could not yet be baptized. Yet, becoming a Catholic in my heart and soul helped to soothe or quell the emptiness and loneliness I had begun to experience. The not knowing where I came from or the circumstances from which I came was unsettling. I knew my mother had not told me the whole truth, but I did not understand why, and there was nothing I could do or say to make her tell me her tightly held secret. Resentment and anger began to build, but in these early years, I was respectful and did not express it.

4 ⌗

California Bound

In early 1955, Aunt Alma and Uncle Earl moved to California to find a better life. That summer, Mother took David and me to California on the Santa Fe Super Chief. Because my mother was the widow of a railroader, David and I got free passes. So we were off to California to see my aunt and uncle. They lived in Hollywood in a small apartment near its famous intersection Hollywood and Vine.

We toured all of the parks, movie lots, *Olvera Street*, City Hall and the beaches. It was an amazing experience for David and me. No two brothers, nine and eleven years old, could have had a better summer.

Our adventures of that summer were life altering. The trip home to Logan was long and sad. Not one of us wanted to leave California, and for the next year we longed to go back. My brother and I lived and re-lived our adventures, both together and alone. The two years in age between us made little difference at that time.

Dragnet and Joe Friday were real for us because we had seen City Hall that was so prominently displayed on the Los Angeles Police Department badges at the opening of the show, and we had visited the studios where these television productions and movies were made. We saw Roy Rogers and Dale Evans in person. Only previously heard on radio or seen on television, these things had come alive for us and we wanted to be a part of it.

As the 1956 school year came to a close, Mother told us that she had been invited to interview in Norwalk, California, and we would take the summer to explore moving to California. Our excitement was beyond containment. Our imaginations ran wild with adventures at the beach, movie stars, what our new house might look like.

The Super Chief could not get to Los Angeles fast enough over the three-day trip. Yet, we had fun telling anybody who would listen that we were moving to California in spite of Mother's admonitions that "nothing is for certain, yet." We arrived late evening on a hot night to be greeted by Aunt Alma and Uncle Earl. Even though we were exhausted, Aunt Alma said, "I'm sure the boys will want to drive by City Hall, just to make sure it is still there."

"Yes, yes! Please!" came our reply. "We might even see Joe Friday."

Uncle Earl circled the building and David and I gaped upward at this lighted symbol of L.A., hoping and dreaming that we would always stay in California, that it would become our new home, our new beginning.

In a few days Aunt Alma and Mother enrolled David and me in swimming classes at the Hollywood community swimming pool. Now twelve years old and a strong swimmer, I became a junior lifeguard, receiving my Red Cross certification and Junior Lifeguard emblem. This was a fabulous experience and amazing growth period. I walked in front of Grauman's Chinese Theatre and saw all of the lights and people. I strolled up and down the streets, confident we were going to live there. Ironically, Hollywood was real to me.

I quickly became friends with actor Robert Taylor's daughter, Judy, who was a senior lifeguard at the pool. She was eighteen, very cute, earthy and fun, and unmercifully teased me about my West Virginia accent, and tagged me with the name "Y'all." Judy loved teasing me about how naïve I was about the ways of the world, especially girls. She repeatedly told me with certainty that I had never been kissed. One afternoon, after the pool closed, she enticed me into the girl's room and kissed me deeply. I struggled to break away, and she laughed tauntingly, teasingly saying "I told you so."

"That, my friend," she said, "was a French kiss. Now you have been kissed."

It was wonderful and wild, exciting and scary. The difference in our ages only excited me all the more. At that moment I loved her for pushing the point.

There was another side to Judy, which I liked very much. She was the daughter of a famous actor, yet she was not pretentious or much interested in talking about her father. I became a bit of a nuisance about wanting to know about her life, to know where she lived, what kind of car she drove, who she dated, and what the parties were like. One afternoon a black limousine pulled up to the main entrance to the pool. The car sat idling with no one getting in or out. As we were closing up the pool for the day, Judy said her father had come to pick her up, and she asked if I would like to meet him.

"Yes," I said, and we walked out to the car together. When the door opened, Robert Taylor was sitting to the left side in the back seat. He greeted Judy warmly and told her to get into the car.

She introduced me to him as her friend, J.P. Judy had started calling me J.P. and I liked it because it sounded more sophisticated or important than John. Her father shook my hand firmly as he said, "Happy to meet you."

Two things struck me. First, he was a beautiful man, well groomed and impeccably dressed. Second, he looked me straight in the eye as he shook my hand. He was clear, concise, appropriate and warm. My heart sank momentarily when the door closed and the darkened window separated us.

Then just as quickly the window came down and Mr. Taylor said, "J.P., Judy would like for you to come and visit us, and perhaps have dinner." I said I would like that, and he responded, "Fine, we will do it," and they drove off. It was a wonderful, exciting moment. I had met a movie star and he had invited me to his home!

There was another wonderful discovery that summer, one my mother did not like. There were Roman Catholic churches everywhere. About two blocks from where we lived was Christ the King parish. It was more ornate and beautiful than anything I had ever seen. I spent hours there, sitting, looking, praying, thinking and wishing to be a part of this remarkable and amazing faith.

On Hollywood Boulevard, there was an even more grand church known as Blessed Sacrament. I loved its cavernous design, gold and mosaic art. It was a refreshing place for me, in a literal as well as metaphorical sense. Summers were hot, and walking into the cool, dense sanctuary quieted my soul and body. There was no other place in my life that I had felt such peace. I knew God was truly present in those churches. California was where I wanted to be.

Mother interviewed for the job in Norwalk school district with several people over a week or two and was finally notified that she would begin in August. We were elated and immediately began looking for a home. We found a lovely house in La Mirada that would house us all including my aunt and uncle. We became neighbors to Joseph and Virginia Gerry. Mr. Gerry was an FBI Agent assigned to the Los Angeles Division. They had four boys, and I quickly made friends with Joe Jr. This was a warm and happy home with a strong father and a mother who was a stay-at-home mom.

Virginia could only be described as a "cool mom," intelligent, pretty, athletic and self-assured. She ferried her sons back and forth to swim practice every day and invited me to tag along. I soon became a member of their family and the Blue Fin Swim Club. Many of our Saturdays and Sundays were spent attending swim meets throughout the Los Angeles basin.

The Gerrys were devout Roman Catholics and, much to my mother's chagrin, I often attended church with them. Joe Jr., almost two years older than I, was a significant influence on me, introducing me to the discipline of studying and amateur radio. His parents were very strict about academic achievement and required all of their children to make good grades in order to participate in their hobbies and sports.

Mr. Gerry rarely spoke of his work with the FBI, but it was obvious from his demeanor and dedication to long hours that he was proud to be an FBI Agent. An autographed picture dedicated to Mr. Gerry by J. Edgar Hoover hung in a prominent place at the entrance of their home.

I greatly admired Virginia and Joe Sr. and their family life with the focus on the boys and their activities. Their family seemed complete and normal, almost Ozzie and Harriet like. I somehow knew that, as hard as my mother worked and tried to make a home for David and me, there was something lacking, and it was a father. I did not think of this as painful but, rather, a sad reminder that I had no father.

At the end of the school year, my mother was interviewed and then hired for a better-paying position in the Downey school district. This was a painful move because it took me away from the Gerry family. Not having a driver's license prevented any real further contact as we moved away to Downey, nearly 50 miles. I started Downey Senior High School in the fall. Now, as a ninth-grader, I made a decision to really change my name from John to J.P. A year to one and a half years younger than my classmates, I wanted to somehow appear to be older. Judy Taylor's calling me J.P. seemed to fit my plan.

Downey Senior High was enormous, some 4,000 students, but I soon was connected to a group of swimmers and trying out for the high school's team. I also enrolled in a speech and drama class taught by Mr. Arthur Williams. Taking this class as an elective, I thought it would be an easy A. I was greatly mistaken. Mr. Williams was an extraordinarily demanding teacher and proved to be my nemesis for a time. Each time I failed to live up to his standards or turned in an incomplete assignment, Mr. Williams would confront me head-on. Confrontation was his forte, and I soon discovered he would tolerate nothing but the best you could give either in performance or in a speech. Public humiliation was his specialty, especially if he felt you were not doing your best.

During one class, Mr. Williams asked if anyone could fence. I raised my hand and said that I could. He asked if I had a mask, vest and foil. I said that I did. Actually, the equipment belonged to a friend who had introduced me to fencing. Mr. Williams asked me to bring them to our next class. He then announced we were going to perform a one-act play that involved a fencing scene. Next to our classroom was a small theater-in-the-round, which was used for play rehearsals and student presentations.

The next day I appeared in class with the fencing gear. After some discussion we adjourned to the theater, where Mr. Williams told me I was about to try out for the lead but I had to successfully fence against him. Before we started, he asked if I had fenced much, and I told him and the class that I had taken a few lessons and could hold my own. In about thirty seconds, I learned that Mr. Williams was an exceptional fencer as he beat me about the head and shoulders with his foil. I retired immediately. He asked me to remain after class.

Mr. Williams told me what I already knew, which was that I knew little to nothing about fencing. But rather than ridicule me, he asked if I would like to learn to fence and proposed that if I were willing to learn, he would teach me. I found myself saying yes before I knew the rest of the story, which was that if I reached an acceptable level of skill, I would also have to perform the lead in the play. Then I got nervous. I had no interest in being the lead in any play, especially appearing before the general public, before whom this play was to be acted. I began to protest, and he insisted I had already agreed and that was that.

Arthur Williams proved to be the best teacher I ever had but, true to character, the toughest. As it turned out, I became one of his biggest fans and took classes with him for four years. A devout Roman Catholic with eleven children and a flare for drama and speech-making, he was a formidable personality. What I liked most about him was that he seemed unafraid and would share with our classes his personal and private beliefs and convictions as if we were his peers rather than his students. Still, when it came to our assignments, he cut no slack.

Mr. Williams introduced us to Shakespeare's *Macbeth, King Lear* and his sonnets. We studied great American literature, and it was here that I discovered Ernest Hemingway. I first read *For Whom the Bell Tolls, The Old Man and the Sea,* and then, finally, *Death in the Afternoon.* I was mesmerized by *Death in the Afternoon* and I soon began reading every book in our library I could find on bullfighting.

As the Spaniards would say, I was bitten by the bullfighting bug.

Angus McNab's classical work, *Fighting Bulls*, became my primer because his explanations of the technical aspects of bullfighting and bull breeding were superior. Though I had never seen a bullfight in person, I somehow discovered that bullfights were broadcast on local feed from Mexican television and I watched at every opportunity.

My aunt fashioned a homemade cape out of some material we had around the house. We dyed it red. Even though it was not anywhere close to the weight of a professional cape, the shape was good. I practiced in our backyard almost every day. Like shadow boxing, I would imagine a bull charging me and I would make the passes I had seen on film or in illustrations.

*****

Shortly after my fourteenth birthday, I became ill and stayed home for a few days, until my appendix ruptured. Fortunately, my mother came home early from school to check on me and realized something serious had happened. She got me in the car and took me to my uncle's home shortly before he was to start his afternoon office hours. He was a Cuban-born general surgeon who had a huge medical and surgical practice in East Los Angeles.

While I was lying on the sofa in his den, he gently pressed on the right side of my abdomen, and I painfully drew my knees to my chest. He immediately called the hospital to prepare for an emergency appendectomy. As he and my mother helped me up to head for the car, he coldly asked my mother why she had taken so long to get me to him. I had been sick for three days, and she thought it was just a mild stomach virus.

I was on the critical list for fourteen days, with constant care by my uncle and a nurse by the name of Amy Cisneros. For much of the time I was under an oxygen tent and delirious from pain and medications. I recall my mother tearfully telling me they might lose me. She told me to pray hard. The nights were the hardest for me, and I constantly tugged at or pulled out the tube that had run into my stomach through my nose.

The solution to the problem was that Amy Cisneros sat and held my hand throughout the night. This remedy quieted me and set me on a road to recovery. Once the oxygen was discontinued and I could begin to tolerate liquids and soft foods, my time in the hospital came to a close. I returned to school now one month behind.

*****

Surviving the ruptured appendix stirred in me a desire to work in the hospital. I soon spoke to my uncle about the possibility of arranging some part-time work for me. He insisted that I was too young and the most important thing I could do was to finish school before even thinking about a job. I was not deterred.

Downey Community Hospital was two blocks from my high school. I filled out an application, lying about my age and forging a work permit, and soon was hired as an orderly trainee. I was allowed to work two hours in the afternoon on school days and four hours on Saturday and Sunday.

Under the supervision of the charge nurse, I was trained to take temperatures, pulses and blood pressures. At the beginning of our shift, it was my job to take vital signs and record them. I then assisted with bed pans and urinals as needed and got folks ready for dinner and served their trays. Always cheating on the time a bit, I would leave the hospital at about 5:30 or 6 p.m. and head for home. I was paid a dollar an hour.

This work excited me beyond anything I could have imagined and I loved it, volunteering for any duty the nursing staff would allow me to take on. The experience opened up a whole new world to me and I began to think seriously about a career in medicine. I could hardly wait for summer so that my hours could be increased. The downside to this new phase of my life was that I left the swim team and other school activities to dedicate myself to the hospital.

Soon I came to the attention of an orthopedic surgeon, Dr. Strong, who saw me gently adjusting a traction setup on a football player who had a compound fracture of the femur. The surgeon remarked kindly about the care I was taking to set up the equipment. He asked if I had ever seen a surgery, and I told him I had not. He commented that perhaps he could arrange for me to observe one of his surgeries if I would care to do that. I eagerly agreed, thinking this would be something easily arranged. Nothing happened for some weeks. Dr. Strong had broached the subject with the operating room nurse supervisor, who had nixed the idea because of my youth.

One Friday evening as I made my rounds taking temperatures and blood pressures, Dr. Strong saw me in the hallway and asked if I would like to observe a hip replacement the next morning. I told him I would, and he cautioned me not to say anything to anyone. He told me about the nurse supervisor's refusal to allow me in the operating room, but said she would not be on duty Saturday and what she did not know would not hurt her. His surgery was the only case scheduled for Saturday morning.

I slept very little that Friday night. I was at the hospital very early waiting for Dr. Strong.

Changing from civilian clothes into operating room greens, Dr. Strong cautioned me to stay away from the sterile field and if I became woozy from the sight of blood and tissue being cut, I should breathe through my mouth and think about something else. He said that if I became very unsteady I should ask someone in the operating room for an ammonia vial.

I remained outside the operating room while the patient was prepared and listened to Dr. Strong discuss the case with his assistant while they scrubbed their hands clean. I followed them as they entered the room, and I retreated to the corner. I waited there until the patient was draped and completely ready for the opening incision. Dr. Strong invited me to come closer for a better look.

As the bright red blood seemed to flow out of his knife as he made the incision, I was fascinated. As skin, fat and muscle were separated, Dr. Strong explained what he was doing.

I was so enthralled that I had completely forgotten about the possibility of becoming woozy. However, once the hammering and sawing began, I grew faint. I suppose my color was as green as the clothing I was wearing, because someone noticed I was going out for the count.

Before I knew it, a broken vial of ammonia was under my mask and I shook off the fainting spell. The staff had a good laugh and joked about me losing my operating room virginity.

This opportunity to observe a surgery and to see the skill of Dr. Strong put me into a frenzy of learning. I stuck my nose in every change of dressings and took every opportunity I could to sneak into the operating room to observe. I was soon practicing to tie knots and do the stitches with 3.0 silk and chromatic sutures. I learned the names of instruments for retracting, clamping and suturing - *USA, peon, Kelly* - and their names and functions became second nature to me.

I now had two passions: bullfighting and medicine. And strangely enough, they did not seem incompatible or odd to me. While I did not consciously think about the fact that bullfighters suffered all sorts of injuries usually requiring surgery, I believed my new-found skills would be a help to me if I were ever injured in a bull ring. I could not or would not let go of the idea that I could be a bullfighter and somehow work in medicine.

My fifteenth birthday present from my mother was a trip to see my first *corrida* (bullfight) in Tijuana. Jaime Bravo and Fernando de los Reyes, "El Callao," fought that day. While Bravo was the crowd pleaser with his boyish looks and sensational style, there was something so appealing and graceful about the quiet, classical manner of "El Callao," that I left the bullring that day certain I wanted to be a bullfighter like him.

I was soon looking for others who shared my growing passion.

As luck would have it, my family decided to visit the planetarium at Griffith Park on a Saturday afternoon. As we drove through the park up to the planetarium, I noticed a dusty, round clearing about 75 yards off the road, surrounded by trees and low scrub.

There was a small group of men practicing *"running the horns"* and caping those with the horns in mock bullfighting. I became so excited I demanded that my uncle stop the car. As he pulled to the side of the road, and almost before he had come to a complete stop, I sprang from the car and ran over to the area where the bullfighters were practicing.

I silently watched the men. They hardly noticed I was there as they went through their paces, occasionally calling out to the young man running the horns, "Toro, toro, ahah, ahaaha."

Then, the charge would come, slow, smooth. The man running the horns came to the cape just as a real bull would, but slowly. There were nine or ten men there. Some were speaking Spanish, others English. One looked familiar. It was Jaime Bravo, the Mexican matador I had seen in Tijuana, and who, as it turned out, was married to Hollywood actress Ann Robinson. She became famous after her performance in the H.G. Wells film *The War of the Worlds*.

One of the men finally finished his cape work, a beautiful series of classical *veronicas*. He looked up, smiling broadly, and asked if I wanted to try a few passes.

"You bet," I said quickly, only to be stopped in my tracks by my uncle who had come up along my side without my even noticing him.

"We have to go. Get in the car. Your mother does not want to be late for the show at the planetarium."

I protested. He insisted.

As we turned toward the car, one of the bullfighters said, "We are here most Saturdays from about ten until two. Come around if you want to give it a try. I'm Carlos. See you later."

Somehow I managed to get to Griffith Park that next Saturday to find the *toreros* practicing, just as Carlos had said they would be. There were fewer men practicing that day, but I soon learned they were members of a bullfighting club and often went to bullfights in Tijuana, just 100 miles south of Los Angeles.

As it turned out, Carlos was Carlos Chipres Jr., the oldest of three brothers, who had a real passion for bullfighting. His brother Bob (an active duty Marine) also liked bullfighting, while the youngest, Ron, seemed too young and not much interested. The Chipres family was Spanish/Mexican and their ties to their culture and traditions were strong.

Their father, Carlos Sr., born in El Paso, Texas, was a pretty good featherweight boxer in his day, and their mother, Virginia, born in California, carried her Grijalva family name with a lot of pride. The Grijalvas were from Salamanca, Spain. Together they encouraged the boys and took them to see their first bullfight in Tijuana on July 4, 1959. Family outings to Mexico to visit family and see bullfights were common.

After a while, I became one of the family. We practiced our cape work on Saturdays, and traveled to Tijuana to see bullfights on Sundays. Now sixteen and with a driver's license, I practically lived at their house. It was like being adopted again, but knowing why and how it happened.

Saturdays became special because Carlos Sr. would put us to work painting houses in the morning; in the afternoons he would bring an old bullfighter from Tijuana, Chalio, to oversee our training with the capes.

Over the weeks and months of training on our own and with Chalio, my confidence grew, and I began to plan to move to Mexico City. During a meeting of our club, known as *Pena Taurina Hermanos Huerta*, the American bullfighter Jeff Ramsey paid a visit trying to garner some financial support for his efforts in Mexico. Jeff was impressive, knew a great deal about bulls and was trying to break into the profession. He had lived there a number of years and was beginning to get serious opportunities to fight in important bullrings in the provinces.

We talked about my coming to Mexico. Later in the week, I met Jeff at his brother's home, where he was staying, and we took some time to practice mock bullfighting with a cape. He was completely unimpressed by my skills and assured me I would be killed soon if I were to continue on this track. I left our time together deflated but also angry about his certainty that I would never be a bullfighter. Jeff returned to Mexico City and I returned to my planning and training.

Carlos Chipres and I, along with Harry Fulsom, who also aspired to become a bullfighter, trained most Saturdays for hours.

Harry and I were determined to go to Mexico. After some months, Harry departed, and we got occasional letters from him reporting on his training and fighting in and around Mexico City. His letters were encouraging and I wanted more than ever to go there.

*****

Aspiring to be a bullfighter in any country where bulls are fought is no easy task even for the native sons and daughters. Not unlike the life of a priest, the life of a bullfighter is seen as sacrificial. Few walk this path. One gives up a great deal to become a bullfighter. Often your own family and friends, whether they know anything about bullfighting or not, think you have lost your mind or that you are surely on the road to hardship and danger.

Not every Hispano-American likes bullfighting. Nonetheless, in Spain or Mexico, or any other country where bullfighting occurs, the people know it is a hard road because they read the news about the gorings, the disputes over contracts, and how men are driven to fight bulls however little money the bullfighters make or the number of gorings they suffer. If you are a successful bullfighter, however, you might become a national figure, a folk hero.

If you fight bulls without earning a good living, people think of you as a bum who usually must live off of others: wives, girl-friends or family, to support your love and dedication to the bulls. Bullfighting becomes an obsession or an illness. Still, few make it in the bullfighting game. In a recent authoritative English language publication on bullfighting, *Death and the Sun*, Edward Lewine reports that of the eighty-eight active bullfighters in Spain only ten to twelve are superstars or *figuras* earning big money and filling the most important bullrings throughout Spain.

In the mid 1960s, there were a number of us, North Americans, caping calves and fighting bulls throughout Mexico. One notable, John Fulton, had fought with some success in Mexico and had moved on to Spain. John had another artistic talent, which helped him to support himself and pursue bullfighting on a sustained path. He was a terrific illustrator and painter.

Others of us limped along, grabbing every opportunity to fight any kind of a bull that was put in front of us in any *pueblo*, regardless of the dangers or whether we earned any money. The idea was to get experience and build a following or *cartel* as it is known. The more popular a bullfighter becomes, the more money he will make by filling the bullrings.

Robert Ryan, Diego O'Bolger, Jeff Ramsey, Patricia McCormick, Patricia Hayes, and Walter de la Brosse enjoyed some remarkable successes along the way. Family and friends helped all of them to varying degrees. Ryan had real financial commitment from his family and the encouragement of his father. Walter de la Brosse was helped by Mexican matador Jaime Bravo. Jeff Ramsey got a real kick-start with the help of the great Mexican matador Fermin Rivera, but a goring in Puebla set him back a time, and Rivera's attention turned to his son and others he wanted to help.

*****

In my senior year of high school, I began to work evenings as an orderly on a surgical wing of another hospital. Upon graduation, I began training in the operating room as a surgical orderly. These duties did not permit me to assist in any surgery, but I was in the operating room environment, and this provided ample opportunities to learn.

A few months later, I discovered that St. Francis Hospital in Lynwood, California, was starting a surgical technicians training program based on the Navy's training model. The course was designed around an eight-hour day, four hours dedicated to class and four hours in the operating room observing and working to learn instruments and procedures. Only seventeen years old at the time, I had to lie again about my age to apply for the job. I filled out the application and was accepted.

St. Francis Hospital was an 800-bed Catholic hospital with twelve operating suites and an enormous emergency room. The heavy surgical schedule and variety of cases, to include severe trauma from the freeways and industrial plants nearby, was fertile ground for learning. I thrived in this environment as never before and loved the work.

Near the end of the training period, the chief instructor asked to have a word with me. He asked me if I was so naïve as to think that my references would not be checked and that it would not be discovered that I was not yet eighteen years old. I was speechless as I gasped for some relief from what I thought was to come. Certain I would be dismissed, I remained silent.

My instructor realized my fear and said the teaching staff had spoken to the operating room supervisor, Sister Hermina, and together they had decided not to fire me because I had been an exemplary student. He told me if I passed the final exams, Sister Hermina had already decided to offer me a job.

During my free time, I continued to practice bullfighting with the Chipres family, and we made numerous trips back and forth to Tijuana to see bullfights. I continued to work at St. Francis, but I had made a decision to go to Mexico. So my job as a surgical technician became the way for funding my plan.

J. Perry Smith

My homemade cape, learning to make passes - 1960.

Mock bullfighting with friends Robert Chipres and Harry Fulsom "running the horns." We all went on to fight real bulls.

5 ✠

Bullfighter

The Hemingway Period

Mother had always been alarmed by my interest in bullfighting, but she seemed to expect me to eventually come to my senses and make some sort of a career in medicine. She was very proud of my work as an orderly and later as a surgical technician. When I left for Mexico the first time, I tried to leave home by sneaking off in the middle of the night. I left a letter for her explaining my decision, assuring her that I would be fine.

My plan was to wait at my girlfriend's home until the next morning, when Carlos Chipres Sr. was to pick me up for the drive to Tijuana. Mother found me and insisted that I come home to be with her until I left the next morning. She begged me not to leave, but she somehow understood my resolve. Our good-bye the next morning was a terrible, wrenching ordeal. Carlos Sr. arrived on time and, as I made my way to his waiting car, I could not look back. We were soon on the freeway headed south to Tijuana.

The drive went quickly and I was sad, quiet, afraid and elated all at the same time. Once in town, Carlos Sr. had some business to take care of and I waited for him in a cafe on Main Street. When he returned we went to lunch, meeting Chalio and his wife. Then we went to the bus station to buy my ticket ahead of time to ensure I would have a seat. Carlos Sr. gave me the money for the ticket.

Now we had several hours to wait before the bus left and we went to Chalio's house to wait. As we killed time, Chalio asked if I had a money belt for the money I was taking with me. I told him I did not. He then warned me that there were many pickpockets in Mexico City and I should never carry identification or a wallet in my back pocket. He also cautioned me that since I was an obvious foreigner in Mexico, thieves would assume that I would have money and they would try to take it from me.

I showed Chalio the $500 in Traveler's Cheques and the few dollars I had in cash. He told his wife to make a bag I could hang around my neck to conceal the checks and money. Looking at the shape of the folded checks, Chalio's wife quickly stitched together a cloth bag that included a heavy string to cinch or secure the bag so that it could be hung around my neck. This idea worked very well and the bag fit under my clothing, well concealed.

The bus, one of the *Tres Estrellas de Oro* line, departed about 9 p.m., as scheduled, and the long journey to Mexico City began. As I sat somewhere near the middle of the bus, I was befriended by a couple and their teenage daughter as the initial hours passed. In my rudimentary Spanish, I learned they were traveling to Mexico City and then on to Tampico, where they lived. I found them to be kind-hearted and gentle people who were curious as to why an eighteen-year-old American would want to be a bullfighter. They were not horrified by the idea as were some of my friends, but puzzled as to how this could happen. They knew enough about the United States and our culture to know this was a very unlikely profession for a *gringo.*

The three days of travel were exhausting. Yet, I found the trip exhilarating because of the contrasts in the people and geography. They were stunning and beautiful. I loved everything I saw and every conversation I had, and I could never have been more excited.

One of the most memorable moments of the trip was our late-night arrival into Mexico City. As the bus climbed to the rim of the mountains that surrounded the city and began its descent into the valley, the cascade of lights across the bottom of the valley were spread out like the Milky Way itself. It was incredible! Six million people lived there then.

We arrived at the bus station in central Mexico City at about 2 a.m., and my new found friends helped me to get my meager belongings off the bus and find a taxi. I had only Jeff Ramsey's address as a reference. Bidding my friends good-bye, I got into the taxi and gave the chauffeur a piece of paper with the notation: Amsterdam Number 30, *Colonia Condesa.* We arrived within a half hour. I asked the driver to wait while I rang the doorbell at Jeff's boardinghouse.

My attempts to rouse Jeff failed, and I was greeted by obscenities from someone on the second floor and told to go away. My insistence got only further verbal abuse and threats. I retreated to the cab and asked the *taxista* if there was a nearby hotel. Fortunately, there was one about a block away. After the usual registration, I settled into my bed at about 3:30 a.m.

Sometime later in the morning, well after the city had awakened, I got up in somewhat of a daze. After finding breakfast and trying to get my bearings, I returned to Jeff's boardinghouse. There, a maid answered the door and, after some discussion, told me Jeff would not return until about 1:30 p.m. I decided to wait on a nearby bench in a park-like area. At about 1:30, Jeff approached with his bullfighting equipment folded and tucked under his arm. He was completely surprised to see me but welcomed me in and we talked. He introduced me to the landlady and she agreed to let me board there for $40 a month. It was within my budget, or so I thought.

*****

Jeff showed me the ropes and we began training together at a park known as *Viveros de Coyoacan* with a number of other aspiring bullfighters. Our days began with breakfast, which was usually eggs, milk, bread and coffee. Then we took a bus trip out to *Coyoacan* and a short walk to the interior of the park area, where we met with the other bullfighters. From 8:30 or 9 in the morning until about 1 p.m., we would practice our large and small cape work, each of us taking a turn at pretending to be the bull. As a newcomer, I had to learn how to be the bull and act like a bull would act as it came to be passed with a cape. It wasn't long before I was in excellent physical shape. The large cape weighed more than fifteen pounds, and the hours spent with it hardened the shoulders and arms as well as the waist.

I soon learned that competition to get contracts for fights was intense and complicated. Dr. Gaona controlled the largest bullring in the world, *La Plaza Mexico*, as well as a number of other bullrings throughout Mexico. Long lines of aspiring and well-known bullfighters would try to get in to see him at his office in the early evening. It was all part of the ritual and business of getting opportunities to fight.

I wanted to try to see Gaona because I had met him in Tijuana during a *sorteo*, the pairing and drawing by the matadors of the bulls to be found that day, and I was sure he would remember me. Jeff dismissed my goal as absurd because I had nothing to show Gaona such as photographs of me performing in the ring, and Gaona, according to Jeff, would no more remember me than the man in the moon.

Over the next eight or nine months, I began to meet other bullfighters who trained at *La Plaza Mexico*. Some of them invited me to train with them there. Jeff dismissed them as a bunch of has-beens and worthless bums. When I asked why we were not training at *La Plaza Mexico*, he became condescending and said, "There is nothing to be gained." He would not discuss the matter further.

It was during this time that I met Victor Pastor, who then introduced me to a fellow American from Tucson, Jim Bolger, who later became Diego O'Bolger. Diego was amiable and charming, a practicing Roman Catholic, and seemed much more willing to help me get started as a bullfighter. I told Jeff of my intentions to start training at *La Plaza Mexico*. He was furious because he thought I should continue to train with him and listen to his advice. Our relationship became cold and distant. I began to look for another place to live.

Soon after, Diego's landlady had a vacancy in her boardinghouse, and I jumped at the opportunity to take the room, even though it was $45 a month. The food was better, the landlady was easier to get along with and Diego and I got on very well.

Training in *La Plaza Mexico* was the highlight of my day. Every time I approached this cathedral-like structure with its life-sized bronzes of the greatest icons of the bullfighting world, I was in awe of its grandeur and importance, always mindful of the triumphs and tragedies of the men who fought there. I loved walking by the corrals where the bulls were held, looking down at them, as mystical, ancient beasts, beautiful and powerful. Some days I would sit for hours watching them after they had been off-loaded from the special trucks that brought them from the ranches, awaiting their destiny the following Sunday.

My life was now about fighting bulls and the daily grind of trying to make it happen. As it is in most professions, you cannot do it alone. Friends must be made and deals must be cut. Despite being as romantic a notion or adventure as I thought it might be, bullfighting, like every other business, is about making money. Nonetheless, I kept trying and, through my new friendships, found a few opportunities to fight on bull ranches during *tientas (the testing of calves)*. I also appeared twice in the Nogales, Sonora bullring, and once in Chetumal.

Chetumal, Yucatan

"Hey, *gringo*, I thought you were going to die."

"Where am I? What happened?" I weakly asked as I awoke out of the fog of a long sleep or dream, trying to focus and understand my circumstances.

"Your bull hit you hard and threw you to the ground. You have been out for a long time, almost a whole day. You have a big concussion. I thought you might die."

"Please don't say that again. You are scaring me," I said with a little more energy. "Do I have a *cornada*, a goring?"

My attendant said almost cheerfully, "No, you will have to wait for another bull to give you your *bautismo de sangre.*"

"My baptism of blood," I thought. It is what the bull world calls the first goring of a bullfighter.

"You are going to be alright now, I think," he continued. "You are in my little clinic. I am Dr. Sanchez, at your service," he said almost formally. He was dressed in a filthy white coat and open collar shirt, and smelled of sweat and booze… and as he turned to walk away I realized he was drunk!

"When can I get out of here?" I asked hurriedly.

"I don't know yet," he replied and he headed for the door. "By the way, your friend, the other *torero*, is waiting to see you. I will tell him to come in."

Victor appeared almost immediately and asked how I felt. He said the bull hit me high in the chest and my arms fell over his horns. With a jerk of the bull's head I went flying through the air some fifteen feet and crashed into the *barrera*, or fence.

"How long have I been here?"

Victor said I was moved from the bullring to Dr. Sanchez' clinic almost immediately after being tossed.

"You have been unconscious for about eight hours. Since we don't have any money and this was a *pachanga* (a non-union, informal bullfight), we are in this shit-hole clinic."

"You have to get me out of here, now." I said. I tried to move, but I was strapped to the gurney, still in the pants of my fighting suit. My jacket was lying in a heap in the corner with whatever other clothing had been removed. Still wearing my undershirt, I was soaked in sweat and the grime of dried blood and dirt.

Victor helped me sit up and we hit the single light bulb hanging overhead as he brought me upright. The swaying of the light, casting a shadow on the wall of the infirmary, made me sick to my stomach, causing me to dry heave. I had not eaten for about sixteen hours.

Dr. Sanchez came into the room, and asked how I was feeling. I said that I wanted to go home, back to Mexico City.

"That's a twenty-four hour bus ride; you better rest here a while longer. You should take it easy now."

"We have to go. I can't pay you," I said.

"Oh, I know. I am helping you because you are a *torero* and I like bullfighting. All of you novices are poor. I don't expect anything. When you get famous and start making money, then you can pay me," he said, smiling at his little jab of sarcasm.

I could barely walk as Victor and I made our way to the bus station. He somehow managed our baggage and fighting equipment. Once at the station we waited for what seemed an eternity. Yucatan was relentlessly hot and humid and the stench from the crowd in the terminal was horrific with no relief anywhere from either the heat or the hordes. As a bus would depart more people would just show up, replacing the sweating, odorous bodies that had just left.

We were famished and with only a few pesos between us, we decided to buy some bread, fresh orange juice and coffee. Wolfing down our meager provisions, we smiled at each other for the first time in days.

We had made it. We had survived an afternoon of facing half-caste bulls, *criollo* stock known as *zebu*, in a crummy backwater bullring with nothing but a concussion, bumps and bruises to show for it. We were happy and we were on our way home.

November 22, 1963

I had returned from my daily training session at *La Plaza Mexico* and, having had lunch, I was taking a nap. There was a knock on my door. Before I was completely awake and up to answer, a *gringo* opened the door and stepped into my room.

He said, "I'm looking for Diego. Your landlady told me he is out of town, but you are a friend of his."

A little surprised by the intrusion, I looked at this well-dressed, poised man and said, "Who are you?"

Rather than answering my question, he asked, "Do you know the president has been shot?"

Not completely understanding his meaning, I said, "What did you say?"

"The president has been shot," he repeated.

"What president?" I asked.

"Our president," he said. "President Kennedy has been shot."

I was so stunned that I was at a complete loss for words and had no idea what to say or do next. There was no television in our boardinghouse, and I had no radio to listen to the news although the landlady had turned on her radio, having learned from the intruder about President Kennedy's assassination.

Somewhat recovered from the shock, I asked again, "Who are

you?"

"I am Carl Koller, a friend of Diego's."

I asked him to sit down and tell me what he knew about the Kennedy shooting. Carl said he had heard the news on the street. Now he wanted to get back to his hotel to watch television to get a better sense of what was happening.

Somewhere in the dialogue he asked what I was doing in Mexico, and I told him that I was a *torero*.

"Oh, no, not another one." He laughed and said, "Well, then, like Diego, you must be starving."

Then he asked if I would like to come to his hotel to watch the news and later get some dinner together. "My invitation," he said, indicating clearly he would pay. Looking at me in my jeans and a t-shirt, he asked if I had a coat and tie to dress up for dinner. I told him I did not own a dress coat much less a tie.

Taking charge immediately, Carl said, "We are about the same size. I have a jacket that will fit you and a tie you can wear. I'm happy to loan them to you."

Leaving my boarding house, Carl hailed a cab, and we went to the *Zona Rosa*, a popular, upscale shopping, restaurant and hotel area in Mexico City. He was staying at one of the best hotels there, the *Maria Isabella*. Immediately upon entering his room, Carl turned on the television and ordered room service for drinks and some appetizers. No U.S. feed of news was available, so we watched Mexican newscasters talk about the assassination for several hours.

I felt sick and I wanted to go home to California, but I had no money to call home nor did I have enough money to travel. All contact with my mother was by mail or telegram, so I was cut off from my family in the States. I felt a tremendous sense of loss and isolation. I needed to feel safe.

Carl and I ate dinner in the hotel restaurant, which was elegant and the food was exceptional. It was the first time in my life that I had eaten fresh grilled shrimp in combination with steak. I thought it was the best meal I had ever eaten.

Carl told me his story and why he was in Mexico. He was the regional sales representative to Miles Laboratories, the maker of Alka Seltzer. He also was dating a Mexican woman, Blanca Maria Lucio. As it turned out, he was to see Blanca Maria and her family over the weekend and he asked if I might like to go with him for a family outing. The idea delighted me and I accepted immediately.

The next week was filled with the mourning of President Kennedy. Mexico and much of the rest of Latin America loved him, and especially his Jackie. Easily recognized as a *gringo* or North American, I was frequently stopped on the street by total strangers who tearfully expressed their condolences. It was overwhelming and I kept wondering what would happen to my country. It felt strange not to be in the United States.

*****

Over the next weeks, Carl and I became friends, and he began to try to persuade me to quit "chasing the bulls." He suggested that I start school at Mexico City College, then located on the road from the flower market in Mexico City to Toluca. With no prospects for employment and no working papers, the idea seemed far-fetched. In truth, I was not much interested in giving up my attempts to become a bullfighter, but I listened because I knew Carl was sincere and he had been kind and generous.

As the weeks and months passed, Carl came in and out of Mexico City for his business. We became even closer because I had started to date Blanca Maria's sister, Gloria.

It was during this time that Carl introduced me to Edris Rice-Wray, M.D. Always impeccably dressed and coifed, Dr. Rice-Wray was a small woman with a formality and correctness about her that demanded attention and respect. She survived polio at a young age and walked with a noticeable limp. One of the few women doctors of her time, she was conducting field testing for birth control pills.

Dr. Rice-Wray had conducted similar field work in India and Puerto Rico before coming to Mexico and she was the subject of considerable controversy because of her research. The Mexican Catholic Church publicly denounced Dr. Rice-Wray in its opposition to her work. Anonymity and free pills were given to the women who came to her clinic, and their husbands may or may not have known these women were on birth control pills. Dr. Rice-Wray would receive anonymous threats and harassing phone calls and there was the occasional vandalism at her clinic, especially after her work was discussed in the press or otherwise publicized.

Dr. Rice-Wray hired me as her personal assistant and chauffeur. We spent many hours together in Mexico City's horrendous traffic, and I became close to her family as we got to know each other. A Mexican physician associated with Dr. Rice-Wray befriended me, and since I had surgical technician skills, he asked me to assist him at a charitable maternity clinic where he worked some evenings and on the weekends.

This clinic served Mexican-Indian women who had little or no prenatal care. They walked into the clinic and climbed onto a table and into stirrups to deliver their babies. Compared to my experience in the operating and delivery rooms in California, I found this clinic so basic as to be crude and dangerous, yet it was better than having the women give birth in the street. At least in this clinic they and their newborns had a better than even chance of surviving, if there were no serious complications. We did occasionally lose a child, mostly breaches and stillborns.

I rebelled against these deaths because I believed they were usually a result of poverty and lack of education. These were the poorest of the Indians and few cared about them. Somehow I knew these circumstances, and especially these deaths, diminished us all.

The demands on my time began to erode my training at the bullring. I enjoyed working for Dr. Rice-Wray. She also encouraged me to go to Mexico City College, and offered to pay the tuition. I accepted her offer and began classes, but I also continued to train at *La Plaza Mexico* intermittently. I could not give up the dream of becoming a bullfighter.

Diego had introduced me to St. Patrick's Roman Catholic Church in *Colonia Tacubaya* and Father Dunstan Stout, O.P., the assistant rector. St Patrick's served the English speaking community of Mexico City. I attended there about a year and I became close to Father Dunstan. I told him about my life-long desire to become Catholic and after three months of instruction in the Catholic faith, he baptized me on January 16, 1964, at St. Patrick's. My sponsors were Gloria's parents, Manuel and Concepcion Lucio Arguelles.

It was one of the happiest days of my life with much ceremony and rejoicing with the entire family. They presented me with a solid gold medal and chain depicting the face of Jesus, crucified and crowned with thorns. It was one of the most beautiful gifts I have ever received, perhaps because Manuel gave it in celebration and with considerable emotion and pomp. I was overjoyed.

A Call from Home

Life in Mexico was better for me during this time. I loved living there and my ever-increasing circle of friends was encouraging and supportive. Then, out of the blue, I received a telegram from my Aunt Alma asking me to come home as soon as I could get there. Her message was short and to the point - my mother was seriously ill and likely to die. Upon hearing my news, Dr. Rice-Wray paid for my airline ticket from Mexico City to Los Angeles. I flew home the next day.

I arrived in the early evening. Aunt Alma met me at Los Angeles International and took me directly to Mission Hospital in Huntington Park to see Mother. Arriving at the hospital, I found her in a semi-coma with a fever of 104 degrees. She was delirious and not able to communicate except with moans between her interrupted breathing. I spoke to the head nurse, whom I knew from my previous work at the hospital.

"As a matter of fact," she said, "Your mother's situation is dire and there is not much we can do for her except to make her comfortable." I asked to see the chart, and she refused.

When I asked for a diagnosis, she sarcastically asked, "Which one would you like?" I told her I was alarmed by Mother's high fever and wanted an explanation as to the cause.

She said, "Your mother is compromised by arterial sclerosis, diabetes, congestive heart failure and obviously some sort of infection. What else can I tell you?"

I told her we somehow had to get the fever down, and she told me to allow the staff to care for my mother.

I was puzzled by what I perceived as hostility and resistance to my inquiries. I wondered if my past experiences with this nurse had been lacking in some way. I decided to take things into my own hands and found my way to the ice machine. Packing my mother's body with ice would reduce her fever. As I passed by the nurses' station, I overheard the nurse talking to Mother's doctor, telling him that he needed to come to the hospital to stop my interference with my mother's care. I continued with my plan. About an hour later, Dr. Winter appeared, and he asked me to come to the doctors' lounge to talk about Mother's condition.

Dr. Winter repeated much of the nurse's comments and reiterated that my mother had little chance of recovery. "So we write her off," I angrily said. "You want me to stand by and watch, doing nothing about her fever?" Dr. Winter explained that the source of the infection was not known but that he was treating her with the strongest antibiotics available and we needed to give them time to work. The cold, moist ice packs would help, but we had to be careful not to reduce her body temperature too quickly. He suggested I go home to rest and we would talk again in the morning. I agreed.

Morning came after a fitful and restless night and I made my way to the hospital. By midday, Mother's fever had broken, and she was lucid. Over the next five days, I rarely left the hospital, staying close to her to ensure her care continued and helping, as I knew how. Aunt Alma, Uncle Earl and David visited every afternoon. My friends from the hospital staff came by often and expressed their concern. By the fifth day, Mother's condition was critical and Dr. Winter thought her death was imminent. He suggested that, if Mother and I had any unfinished business, it should be taken care of that day.

At about 4 p.m., Mother seemed to rally and became quite animated. I said, "Mother, you are about to die and you are going to leave me alone. Please tell me about my adoption. I need to know who my parents were."

She answered, "John, leave this thing alone. It will only hurt you." She paused for some seconds, and then said with resolve, "I am your mother, and I have loved you as no other mother could. You are mine, nothing else matters."

Suddenly she teared up and said, "There is something I need to tell you about your father, John. Your father had a long-time affair with a woman in Chattanooga, Tennessee. You remember that he ran the trains between Danville and Chattanooga for many years. He met this woman there and saw her when he went to Chattanooga. This was very hurtful for me, but there was nothing I could do about it, so I tolerated it. I want you to promise me that you will never do this to the woman you marry."

Mother refused to tell me who the woman was and how she knew about the affair, saying it was not important. I wondered if this woman might be my biological mother.

She then asked me for another promise, which was that I would give up bullfighting and come home to California to take care of my brother, David. I did not answer because I was so stunned by her refusal to talk about my adoption and the story about my father. We just held hands for a long time. She became quiet, closed her eyes, her breathing eased and she slipped into death.

I left the room, and as I walked by the nurses' station I told the charge nurse my mother was dead. I asked her to notify my Aunt Alma, who would know what final arrangements needed to be made. I left the hospital and went home without saying anything to anyone else.

Mother's funeral was a blur, but we all somehow got through it. I spent the next few days completely withdrawn and very angry. I had no explanation for anyone, even though my family and friends expressed concerns about me. I asked my Uncle Orlando to intervene at his hospital to find work for me. During our discussion, I mentioned to him that I was having trouble sleeping and I was exhausted. He told me this was a result of my grief, and he prescribed a mild sleeping medication. I continued to be withdrawn and focused only on going to work for a few weeks to earn enough money to return to Mexico.

St. Patrick's Church - The Dunstan Factor

Mother died April 16, 1964 of septicemia. I was nineteen. Aunt Alma assumed custody of David and she decided to take David, and her husband, Earl, back to Logan, West Virginia, because Uncle Earl was suffering from advanced black lung and wanted to go home to die. Working just long enough to make the money I needed, I returned to Mexico City to continue my life as an aspiring bullfighter.

After the long bus trip from Tijuana to Mexico City, I settled

back into the routine of going to *La Plaza Mexico* to train with my
fellow *toreros* and spend the evenings talking with bullring *impresa-
rios* to get a fight in an important bullring in or near Mexico City or
Guadalajara. A successful fight in one of these bullrings would open
up opportunities throughout Mexico.

I also continued to see my sweetheart, Gloria Lucio, whose father had made it abundantly clear that I had better start college and
find some responsible work, "other than a bum's life of bullfighting," if I wanted to be taken as a serious suitor.

Things were unraveling for me. I was getting nowhere with
bullfighting and I was broke with few prospects of making enough
money to live since Mexican work laws were so restrictive for for-
eigners. But then, one beautiful early summer evening, my life was
changed in almost an instant.

It was my custom to go to the Church of St. Patrick in *Tacubaya*, in the late afternoon to be alone and pray. There was a beautiful,
realistic crucifix of Jesus over the altar that always held my attention
as I knelt in the back of the church to pray. The church was cool in
the spring and summer heat. It was at a considerably higher altitude
above the smog of Mexico City, and sunsets could be spectacular,
streaming light in through the sanctuary windows, dancing color all
around.

I had been in the church for some time, not thinking or praying
about anything in particular, yet I was staring intently at the body
of the crucified Jesus on the cross. His body was stretched out and
contorted in pain and I somehow felt one with him in his torture. He
was alone in his agony. I was alone in mine.

Then in a slow agonizing movement, Jesus moved his head

from his one shoulder to the other side of his body where it rested for a while. His eyes opened slightly and he looked at me. I blinked several times thinking I had fallen asleep and I was dreaming. Jesus' head hung to his shoulder as I stared into his face; I expected to hear him cry out or say something to me. The sunlight was now beginning to fade fast and I began to think I had just imagined that Jesus had moved, but just then he moved his head back to the original position. The sun had set and it was finished.

The church was so still I could hear my heart beating. Yet, there was a calm that penetrated my body as I moved from the kneeler and sat back into the pew, not afraid or excited or overjoyed. It was peace--the deepest, most profound assurance that no matter what, God was with me--I was in an indescribable place of serenity. As I rested in this amazing moment, Father Dunstan, my priest and friend, appeared out of the now deepening dusk that had darkened the church.

"How long have you been here?" he asked.

"Not sure," I told him.

"Are you alright?" he wondered. "It is nearly dark. Shouldn't you get home? The last bus runs in a short while."

"Will you hear my confession?" I asked.

"Of course," and we moved to the confession box a few feet away.

I began, "Forgive me, Father, for I have sinned..."

Afterwards, Father Dunstan asked me to stay for dinner, and over soup and bread around the small kitchen table in the priest's living quarters, I told him what had happened earlier in the church. He looked tenderly into my eyes and simply said, "I know." We embraced and I left. We never spoke of it again. There was no need. He, too, had experienced the living, suffering, dying Christ.

Father Dunstan had long thought I should become a priest and he encouraged me to give it a chance. He arranged for me to visit his Passionist order in California when I decided to return there. He also suggested I make a retreat at a sixteenth century Discalced Carmelite Monastery, high in the mountains of central Mexico.

I started my visit at the monastery Thanksgiving week. As the bus climbed higher and higher toward the *pueblo* where the monastery was located, the air became thin and cold. As the handful of Indians and I got off the bus in the town square, I shivered against the cold, no longer having the protection of the bus and the warmth of other body heat. Stupidly, I had not worn proper clothing, but I was grateful to Father Dunstan for having given me a heavy wool cassock to wear at the monastery.

I spent two weeks with the Carmelites, following their daily routine of prayer and work. They allowed me to fully participate in almost every part of their life since they knew I was trying to make a decision about becoming a priest. The days and nights were filled with chanted prayers and masses in Latin, incense and long hours of silent prayer in the choir stalls and main church. The devoted local Indians came and went mixing their ancient pagan rites and Catholicism in ways that seemed incongruent, but in truth, these were real and deep expressions of faith, mystery and culture. It only intensified my experience, and I was swept away by the ritual, rhythm of the monastic day, and apparent holiness of the monks and their dedication to a life of sacrifice and solitude.

I came down from the mountain believing God wanted me to be a priest. Why else would he have revealed himself to me in such an intimate way on his cross in St. Patrick's? Why would I find peace only in prayer, the ceremony and rituals of the church?

My girlfriend Gloria was horrified I would make such a precipitous decision. In her mind it was worse than being a bullfighter. At least, if I were a *torero*, we could be together.

I soon packed my bags and returned to Los Angeles.

Once there I visited the Passionist fathers just as Father Dunstan had wanted. But I loved the Franciscans, Order of the Friars Minor, because of their ubiquitous missions and historical importance to California, and I hoped they would accept me into their novitiate. After an interview by a friar in a downtown Los Angeles parish, I went into the bathroom before I started my trip back to Downey. As I pressed up against the urinal I realized the fixture was marble. Surprised, I began to look around the room and it too was built of beautiful colors of marble, opulent and ornate beyond what any bathroom should be like. This I thought was oddly inconsistent with the vows of poverty, chastity and obedience. Remarkably, given my immaturity, I was offended by the extravagance.

Then and there, I decided if I were going to make a commitment to God to be His priest, I was going to make a real commitment to the religious life. The monks I had read about who were living a strict, truly monastic life were in Kentucky, not far from my adoptive father's birthplace of Danville.

In December, just two months after turning twenty-one, I was standing at the Gatehouse of the Abbey of Gethsemani, Bardstown, Kentucky.

NOGALES, SONORA
BULL RING
Sunday November 3
At 3 P.M.
Bull Fight
Amateur Day

If you are looking for thrills and fun don't miss this festival if you have never seen a bull fight, come and see now tho get ⋅t rted!

TAKING PART IN THIS FESTI- VAL ARE THE ASPIRANTES:

Diego O' Bolger - Dieguin
Perry Smith, Ricardo Vizcaino,
Jim Verner, David Van Hoven
Fightin the Brave Bulls
However they Can

So that everyone can see this bull fight all ⋯ ⋯ ⋯ will be **$2.00**

My first appearance in a major bullring, Nogales,
Sonora, November 3, 1963

The bulls are waiting.

The bulls are ready.

My first paseo in a "suit of lights." Nogales, Sonora,
September, 1963

Day of the Novillero (aspiring bullfighters), Santin, 1962

Performing a "chicuelina" in border town Nogales, Sonora.
Notice the beer price in English

6

Monk

The Merton Factor

"It will take about seven years to get used to the silence," Father Matthew Kelty said, as he took a hard bite into a raw whole onion. He saw my utter surprise that he could enjoy an onion as if it were an apple, and joked that it was his after-supper dessert. I liked Father Matthew. He was relaxed and informal, but his real agenda was to tell me about the life I was about to enter.

Father Matthew was then the vocation director at the Abbey of Gethsemani, the largest and perhaps best-known Cistercian (Trappist) monastery in the world. His job was to tell me that the community had voted with only one dissenting vote to accept me as a postulant. Father Matthew, with a bemused tone, said, "Father Felix voted 'no' because he didn't think we needed a bullfighter in our midst since we have had a number of adventurous types come to the monastery, only to leave when they discovered how hard it was to be quiet."

Father Matthew outlined what was to come. I would remain in the guesthouse for a few days until I could be fitted for the off-white colored habit (or clothing) of a postulant. I would get a monk's haircut - bald. I was to pray and think about what religious name I would like to be known as. It was Benedictine custom to take the name of a saint. "Do not choose a name that a monk now has," Father Matthew said solemnly. I asked if Bernard or Benedict were taken. "Yes," was his quick reply. "This is not going to be easy because most of the common names are taken." I had a name of a saint in mind, but I kept it to myself for the moment.

Father Matthew told me to give him a list of three to five names in descending order of preference by morning. "Go to the novices' library and find one of the many books about the lives of the saints to get some ideas," he said. Then from memory he ran through some of the already taken names. It was going to be hard to select a name with a hundred and fifty monks living at Gethsemani. I hoped I would become known as Crispin, the name of the patron saint of cobblers, shoemakers and leather-workers, and I asked if the name was taken. It was not.

Father Matthew saw the surge of excitement and cautioned, "This is a matter that the abbot takes seriously, and he will ultimately decide what your religious name will be." Little did I know I was about to have my first taste of Trappist discipline and obedience to the will of the abbot.

Father Matthew went on to explain the ceremony of reception. He said a supervisory lay brother would be assigned to help me find my way around the monastery, explain the routine, and get me started with my studies. "The two of you will have permission to speak to one another, but do not abuse the privilege with chit chat."

Father Matthew said that the Novice Master, Father Louis (Thomas Merton), was transitioning to a hermitage away from the main abbey, and Father Baldwin would take his place. He saw my disappointment.

"Many of us came here because of Merton and the influence of his books," he said. "But don't worry, you will see him often and hear his lectures. Dom James Fox (the abbot) has not let Louie completely off the hook. He must come into the abbey to concelebrate mass, take at least one meal, and he will continue to offer lectures and reflections for the community."

It was the first time I had ever heard Thomas Merton referred to as "Louie." I understood the implied familiarity of calling somebody by their nickname, but I was slightly taken aback since we were talking about the most famous Trappist monk and writer in the world. "Louie" seemed almost disrespectful.

Indeed, Thomas Merton had influenced and brought many to Gethsemani with his best seller *The Seven Storey Mountain*, but the Trappists had other writers as well. The romantic style of Father Raymond Flanagan was influential among Catholic readers, and I particularly loved *The Man Who Got Even with God*, which was the story about Brother Joachim, a Texas cowboy, who became a Trappist. Merton was a formidable factor in my decision to try the monastic life. It was his religious quest as a convert, adventurer and intellectual that drew me to Gethsemani. Although I am no intellectual, I thought we were similar, particularly since I was a convert and I had gone off to Mexico to become a bullfighter.

"Please, God, let this be the place and life You intend for me. Let this be my home. Make this my family. Make me a good monk." I prayed constantly for the three days as I waited to be vested in monk's clothing and ceremonially received. I had submitted my list of preferred religious names as Father Matthew had instructed with Crispin at the top. It was a good name, one that was obscure and the name of the patron of a humble profession, shoemakers. I was certain Dom James would see the logic, but I was wrong.

Brother Victor, one of our superiors, came to me in the novices' study area, and told me the abbot had rejected my list and I was to submit another three or so names. There was no explanation. Submit more names. I was angry and confused, but I began again. I didn't like any of the names I found and I told Brother Victor and Father Baldwin so.

Father Baldwin said, "You have the option of letting the abbot pick for you." I rejected the idea and began to search the books of saints again. I didn't want a name like "Louie" or "Charlie" to become my nickname for the rest of my life. It was not dignified enough given the sacrifice the Trappist life demanded. I submitted three more names.

"You will become known as Brother Lawrence and you have the option of spelling your name with a 'w' or a 'u,'" Father Baldwin said plainly. "The abbot has chosen this name because Lawrence is one of the saints named in the canon of the mass, and he likes to have monks remembered in the mass. You will also have a major feast day since Lawrence is an important saint. The last Lawrence at Gethsemani died recently, so you will take this name." I angrily asked why we went through the charade of submitting my preferences in the first place.

Father Baldwin responded gently, "I know this is hard for you to accept because you attach a great deal of importance to names; we all do. The abbot has picked the name for you of an important saint that you will want to read, study and learn about. Make Lawrence your model for your life here. The Trappist life is about discipline and obedience. Let this be your first lesson; accept your new name gracefully."

I sighed audibly, resigned. Father Baldwin asked how I wanted to spell Lawrence. I replied with considerable sarcasm, "With a 'u'; at least that will make my name somewhat distinctive and perhaps no one will ever call me Larry."

The naming was sensitive for me because I had often wondered what my name was before I was adopted, assuming I had been given one. Further, so as to distinguish myself from all the other John Smiths in the world, I had used J.P. in my high school years and Perry in Mexico. Perry was easy for Mexicans to remember because of the Perry Mason television program and the world-renowned singer, Perry Como.

Father Baldwin had another surprise. "You will get your first monk's haircut today before noon prayers, and in preparation for your vesting and reception tomorrow, you will make your confession at 2:15 p.m. Father Felix will be your confessor."

I was absolutely shocked. My confessor was to be the very monk who had voted against my being accepted at Gethsemani. I was so dumbfounded I could not respond, not that it would have made any difference. I was glad I had no major sins to confess to this priest whom I decided I didn't like very much. I thought about the irony of it and the abbot's malicious sense of discipline, but I said nothing and did as I was instructed.

A monk's haircut is a quick, almost comical affair. There was no care taken to ensure symmetry. The days of the monk's tonsure, the wearing of a crown-like haircut simulating Christ's crown of thorns, were gone and completely bald was the haircut for all of the brethren.

My hair was longish, and the monk who cut it missed several long strains just behind my right ear. I could feel them, but I could not see them since no mirror was available. I could not complain and I could not speak to anyone about it. I decided I would forget about them or pull them out by the roots, if they continued to bother me.

Returning from my work assignment at the cow barn later in the afternoon, I showered. While drying off, I noticed a razor and mirror lying on a shelf just above a double row of sinks in the common washroom. The small mirror and safety razor took care of my nagging hairs, but just as I had finished and began to survey my new look, an older monk I had not seen standing on the other side of the row of sinks, said, "It looks good."

I was shocked that I was not alone as I had thought, and further mortified to realize I had been caught being incredibly vain. I was also just as surprised to hear him speak to me. I hurried from the room, leaving the old monk smiling at my embarrassment.

*****

"What do you seek, my brother?" Dom James solemnly asked.

"The mercy of God and of the Order," I said, lying prostrate before him and the brethren assembled in the Chapter Room. It was the simplest of ceremonies, but in some ways, one of the most poignant of my life. It was a new beginning, a new family in a holy place, seeking God, "God Alone."

"God Alone" was the inscription over the gatehouse of the abbey. As I lay prostrate on the floor, I believed it was possible to live for "God Alone" and I earnestly wanted to do just that... or so I thought. I believed it would be possible since I was convinced that the Trappist monk's life of prayer and contemplation were the vehicle that would make it possible. In spite of the admonitions from Father Matthew about the depth and difficulties of the silence, the separation from the world and the loss of opportunities for marriage and children, I was ready to live the rest of my life as a Cistercian monk hidden away with another 150 men in the middle of Kentucky's heartland.

In the early to mid-1960s, before Vatican II reforms were instituted, a monk's day began with rising at 2 a.m. to dress and visit the lavatory. There was barely time to use the potty and brush our teeth before the night prayers, known as Vigils, began at 2:30 in the main church. I never got used to getting up at this hour and I was fatigued much of the time. Some monks would nap during the day, but I could not.

The remainder of the day was filled with common prayer services (Lauds, Terce, Sext, None, Vespers and Compline) which made up the "hours" of the liturgy of the daily office, said and sung each and every day in every Benedictine monastery in the world. St. Benedict called this "Opus Dei," the work of God.

Lectio Divina (divine reading) is an important part of the monastic life. Selected readings, read in snippets throughout the day, were meant to lead the monk to reflection, prayer, praise and thanksgiving. Scripture and the writings of the Church Fathers, such as Thomas Aquinas, as well as well-known modern Catholic theologians, formed the basis of these readings. Our meals were eaten in silence, but the noon meal was punctuated by some reading a monk was assigned to give. Postulants and novices were often assigned to this duty so that their reading (and singing) voices could be heard and judged by the community.

Father Louis (Merton) was fond of calling prayer a monk's job or work. In those early days, I thought he was being flippant since I delighted in being in choir and at prayer and did not think of it as work or my job. I rejoiced and found great peace in our singing or recitation of the psalms, upon which our common prayer was based. In each of the "hours," there was a hymn, the reading of scripture, the prayer for the day and a commemoration of the Blessed Virgin Mary.

My favorite prayers were the last of the day that closed with our singing in Latin of the Marian antiphon, *Salve Regina*.

The church lighting was turned off, and we turned, while standing in our choir stalls, to face the stained glass window high above the main altar. We sang in a deep melodic chant as a spotlight brightened an image of the Virgin Mary in the window. It was profoundly moving for me, albeit romantic and sentimental (some called it hokey), but it never failed to bring tears of joy to my eyes. I was comforted and made to feel safe in this moment of worship. It seemed the Blessed Virgin Mary had replaced my absent mother.

*****

When the monks were not in community prayer, there was work to be done on the farm, in the bakery, the kitchen and on the monastery grounds. The monastery had extensive land holdings and about four hundred cows that had to be milked twice daily. Our cheese production was from the milk. We made fruit cakes for Christmas sales to the public. All these activities, not to mention the royalties from the book sales of Father Louis and Father Raymond, made us self sustaining, if not rich by anyone's definition.

Postulants and novices were given light work details to learn the jobs and the rhythm of the Trappist life. The three to four hours we worked each day usually put us outside with the animals. I was assigned to the cow barn and I enjoyed the work. Milking was done by machine, but moving the cows into position and cleaning up was exhausting at times.

I entered the monastery in the dead of winter and working in the barn on those frozen, dark mornings was surreal, if not a little frightening. I soon discovered I could get some warmth by huddling between two cows as I led them into the milking area.

One morning when I was moving towards the milking machines, one of the stubborn beasts stepped on my foot and would not move off. Although it was painful, I did not cry out to the other monk in the milking barn because of our rule of absolute silence during the night hours. My face must have puffed up from the pain and frustration because the supervising brother laughed out loud when he saw my dilemma. Perhaps he too had had this experience, I thought, as he moved the cow forward and off my now throbbing foot. He was amused...my foot hurt for a week.

When possible everything was done in silence and we used a "signing" system to communicate only as necessary. If the work was complex or if a supervisor gave his permission, we could speak, but silence was the rule of the house. Of course, silence could be broken in case of an emergency such as an injury or fire.

Postulants and novices were given a manual with all of the necessary hand signs we needed for communicating. There were many signs and they had served the monk better in a much less complex world. The new monastic world was filled with complicated machinery and a mail-order business for cheese and fruitcakes. It called for creativity when using the signs. Nonetheless, I learned all the signs in about a week and practiced them on every occasion I could. The novice master told me he had never seen a monk learn the signs so quickly. I told him I was an extrovert and I didn't want to be left out of any "conversation." He smiled.

Conversation occurred during classes and chapter meetings. Chapter meetings took place almost daily and they were used to discuss community business or to hear some news from the outside world. The abbot decided what news we would hear. In those days, there were no newspapers, radio or television for the monks. This was not a big deal since we were so busy throughout the day. Our work was about being quiet and contemplative.

There was one kind of chapter meeting I absolutely detested. It was what was known as the Chapter of Faults. The brethren came together and would "proclaim" another for the overt breaking of the rules of the order of the monastery. For example, it was common for a monk to be proclaimed if he carelessly broke a piece of equipment or something of value. The Rule of St. Benedict stipulates that a monk regard "all the monastic utensils and goods of the monastery as if they were the sacred vessels" (31.10). Anyone who loses or breaks anything must take responsibility for it.

The procedure was simple. A monk would rise and announce to the community: "I proclaim Brother Laurence for carelessly breaking the lawn mower, causing a loss of time and money for repairs." The accused monk would then, without answering the infraction, rise and lay down prostrate in front of the abbot's throne and the whole community to ask for forgiveness and receive the abbot's penance.

The penance for such an offense would be meted out by the abbot and would usually involve eating your soup at supper for three days from a small stool while sitting on the floor. One amazing example of this discipline occurred one day when we filed into the refectory for the noon meal; one of the younger professed (having taken vows) monks was kneeling at the entrance with a large stack of broken dishes piled up in front of him. He looked so sad, and as broken as the dishes that lay before him. He also had to eat his dinner soup from the small stool for a week. I made a decision that day I would never – ever – proclaim another monk for any such accident or mistake.

One of the more absurd proclamations I saw was when an older monk proclaimed another for "slapping a paint brush while painting the library walls, thus disturbing the peace of the house." As the abbot gave out a penance, I remember thinking that I hated – yes, hated – this medieval practice which I thought only contributed to pettiness, and some mean-spiritedness on the part of some of the brethren. I could hardly bear to be in the room during the Chapter of Faults.

Yet, there was another practice I found even more difficult. On Fridays at noon, we all would go in procession to our dormitory, stand at the entrance of our sleeping space, strip bare to our waists, and strike ourselves repeatedly on the shoulders with a short whip, known as a flagellum, in a rhythm and at a pace of the superior closest to you. This self-flagellation was to remind us of Christ's own scourging on the day of his crucifixion.

This practice could be painful, especially if the monk next to you was particularly penitential, and you ended up following his lead. Yet, more than the physical pain, I found it humiliating, and I often thought what Jesus endured had to have been so much worse than what we could ever imitate. I thought we just might be insulting God. Nonetheless, such was the discipline.

The Trappist life is about self-surrender to God, and the Rule of St. Benedict provides the way and discipline. Sleeping on straw mattresses on boards in a common dormitory, living on a vegetarian diet with no fish, meat or eggs (except when ill), penitence and fasting, all pale in comparison to the privation when I began to feel God had abandoned me.

The joy and peace I felt in the first months at Gethsemani were now gone. My confidence in the power of prayer had left me, and the hours of meditation, kneeling on the cold, hard floor of the church, only made me angry. Everything was cold. I felt only a great loneliness. God had become distant and silent. I became increasingly anxious, restless and afraid I might go mad. I was irritated by everything, especially Father Louis' cheerfulness and contentment in his hermitage, which he spoke about often to the community during his Sunday afternoon talks. Yet, I settled in and worked hard to conform mentally and physically to the rigors of the life.

Spring finally came, and on a wonderfully bright, warm Sunday afternoon, Father Louis was up-beat and humorous as he talked his way through some theological point.

Then suddenly he stopped almost in mid-sentence, looked directly at me and said, "Some of us here are frauds. We think we belong here. We want to belong here. But we don't."

Then, as if he had not stopped speaking about his earlier topic, he picked up where he had left off.

I was devastated. I spoke to Father Baldwin, the novice master, and he was reassuring, noting that every monk in the community knew that I had moved into an almost predictable period of feeling abandonment and spiritual sterility.

"Every one of us has been through this," he said gently. "It is sometimes harder for some than others, but we all come to this place in our spiritual development. We all have been praying for you for some time now. If you can bear it for a time, I promise things will get better."

"How long?" I pleaded. "This has been going on for months. How long?"

Father Baldwin replied, "Brother Laurence, you are an unusually sensitive man, and this has come on you earlier than in most cases. God breaks our hearts open so that we can love Him more fully. Think of it as a blessing."

I knew I was finished, but I continued for several weeks, growing all the more restless and impatient with God, the Trappists and their arcane rules, and most of all, myself. I decided Father Baldwin was right. I was being impatient with the rules and myself. Many of the monks flaunted the rules making it easier to conform and stay in the monastery. They were mature and better understood that we are all human and needed to "break out" occasionally. I feared that any infraction of the rules would bring dismissal from the novitiate.

Spring was just beginning, full of sweet smells and new color. One Saturday afternoon, I made my way up to the cow barn for the evening milking, and as I crossed the road that ran in front of the monastery, I was nearly run down by two young women in a red MGB convertible.

They skidded to a stop, smiled brightly at scaring me half to death, and told me they were lost. They asked for directions to some place I had never heard of and showed me a map. Stupidly, I acted as if I were a deaf mute, and signed that I could not speak to them. I approached the passenger who was holding out the map, and I pointed to where they were at that moment.

The passenger asked her friend, as if I weren't standing there, why I didn't talk to them. She said, "They take a vow of silence. He is not allowed to talk."

"What a shame. What a waste. He's too cute to be a monk," her friend replied.

They drove off down the road as fast as they had come up it, noisily waving goodbye, the radio blasting. These two would have been seriously proclaimed in the Chapter of Faults for disturbing the peace of the house, I mused. I walked to the barn smiling broadly for the first time in many months.

Now twenty-one, I had given St. Benedict and his monks nearly fourteen months. I had learned how hard it was to live for "God Alone," even in a place that sets out to bring one closer to God through prayer, sacrifice, fasting, penitence, community and good works. Some important and significant changes were coming to the monastery as a result of Vatican II reforms, which had been undertaken by Pope John XXIII. The pope defined the Vatican II Council's immediate task as renewing the religious life of the church and bringing up to date its teaching, discipline and organization, with the unity of all Christians as the ultimate goal.

At Gethsemani, we had already begun to experiment with chant in English and we had been adjusting to how the mass was said in community by special papal dispensation. The Benedictines had considerable pride in being out in front of the rest of the church in matters of liturgical reform and ascetic practices. Unknown to the postulants and novices, there were plans underway to radically remodel the church itself and to do away with the Chapter of Faults which many of the brethren hated.

In the years that followed, the rules about chatting with other monks, recreation and personal hobbies were relaxed. As Brother Luke said to me during my visit to Gethsemani in 1985, "You left too soon. If you had hung on for a few months, you still might have been here. The life is much easier now…less draconian and medieval."

Yet, I could not have waited another minute, hour or day. I was lonely, felt abandoned and broken in spirit. I believed God had not heard my prayer: "Please Lord, let this be the place and life You intend for me. Let this be my home. Make this my family. Make me a good monk."

Father Louis came to see me off as I waited in the Guest House for the bus to come. I told him of my disappointment and despair.

He said, "Perry, whether in the monastery or in the world out there, life requires a good sense of humor. God certainly has one. He created us, didn't He? I have watched you for some time now, and it occurs to me that you have an underdeveloped sense of humor. Work on that, if you will, and whether you come back here or stay out there, you will be fine."

*****

During the discernment phase of the process a candidate goes through for ordination to Holy Orders in the Episcopal Church, there is a great deal of reflection and journaling required. One of my mentors asked that I write about those persons or circumstances that most influenced my decision to seek ordination. I wrote about the Trappists and Merton. Near the end of the paper I realized for the first time that I really did not like Merton as a person. And I said so in the paper.

Merton often complained about the noise and silliness of fruit-cake making and cheese production. He argued that it distracted all the monks from the real business of contemplation, which in his view was what we were about. Yet, it was Merton and his fame that brought the really serious noise and distraction to Gethsemani. Visitors would show up at all hours asking, or in some extreme cases demanding, to see him for spiritual direction or counsel.

Merton's fame and popularity was such that he had special privileges the rest of us did not enjoy: for example, personal correspondence. We were allowed infrequent letters and any we wrote were given to a superior for review before they were posted and sent. Merton had no such restriction. He corresponded with many friends, editors, like-minded writers and monks throughout the world. It can be argued that his correspondence was necessary for his work as a writer, but it did rub some the wrong way.

Merton also had frequent visitors officially permitted by the Abbot Dom James. Some others just happened by, and when Merton was in his hermitage about a mile from the main monastery, there was no way of monitoring his activities. He enjoyed a camera to record some of the visits by friends or other notables. He was fond of entertaining his closest friends with wine, cheese and bread. There was nothing wrong in that, but no other monk had such opportunity or permission to do so.

Thomas Merton was the most eloquent spokesman for the journey and vocational call of the monk into solitude, yet he could not resist the attention and adulation of his admirers and friends. In fact, I think he loved the attention and fame he brought to himself and Gethsemani. He was a genius. He knew it and so did everyone else. He deserved the attention he got, but the paradox was his relentless pursuit of greater and greater solitude; thus his quest to be in the hermitage.

It was, however, in the writing of my ordination discernment paper that I discovered a similarity we shared. In January 1982, *Cleveland Magazine* did a feature article about me and a bank robber I had captured in a revolving door as he tried to run from the bank. In the article, the author was trying to capture something of the essence of my personality, which he had perceived as arrogant. He wrote, "Despite the quiet manner, the soothing voice, I have the vague feeling that what he really wants is his presence announced by a battery of 24 trumpets." It was true.

I was offended by Merton's observations about me, even though he was right in both instances when he directed his comments to me about not belonging at Gethsemani, and when he told me I had an underdeveloped sense of humor. He really had no right to say anything to me. He was a monk who had elected to step down as a superior, Novice Master, and had retreated to the woods. He was presumptuous and arrogant.

Yet, I knew we were similar in at least one facet of our makeup. We both had an intense desire to find God and ourselves in silence and contemplation..."God Alone," as it were. It was our preferred and well-articulated intention to try this path rather than another. Yet, the temptation of clamorous recognition was so intoxicating and alluring.

Merton could not and did not resist it, even to the end of his life. On October 20, 1968, Merton died by accidental electrocution in his hotel room in Bangkok, Thailand, where he had been participating in a conference about Eastern and Western monasticism.

I had come to monastery looking for a family and a place to belong. My mother had died. I was essentially alone. I was grief-stricken, lonely and aimless when I arrived and when I departed Gethsemani. It is said about the monastic life that if you come to the monastery running from something, you will not escape it. In fact, whatever it is a monk might try to run from, it is the very thing that will run into him head on. It certainly was true in my case.

Oddly enough, Merton's suggestion that I develop a better sense of humor has become a life goal for me and I am still working on it. Yet, I am happiest when I am alone in prayer and the contemplation of God, particularly at the moment of the breaking of bread (the moment of fraction) in the Holy Eucharist. I tell myself that it is not about me, it is about God and His Church. Yet, I know, in the deepest part of my being, that it is also about the battery of 24 trumpets announcing my presence... my participation in the parade. Ironically, bullfights and celebrations of mass or Eucharist start with ritual dressing in ornate, special clothing... and a grand parade.

God forgive me, but I do love a parade.

The Abbey of Gethsemani prior to renovations in the 1970s

Vietnam

The 9th Infantry

The monks wasted no time in notifying my draft board of my departure from the monastery, thus ending my deferment. Three weeks after leaving Gethsemani I was notified to report for induction. I went to the U.S. Army recruiting depot in Ashland, Kentucky, since it was not far from where I was staying with a distant relative.

For some reason unknown to me to this day, among the four major military services, I decided the Army was the best choice for me. This recruiting station was an enormous hub of activity with 17- and 18-year-olds pouring out of Appalachia to build up President Johnson's troop increases for Vietnam. As I moved through the various lines for IQ and aptitude tests, and finally a physical examination, I was struck by the sheer numbers and undercurrents of controlled chaos. It was a shock to my system after the quiet of the monastery.

"Smith, John P., Smith, John P.," and then louder, "Smith, John P.," the corporal called out as he walked among the throng of us who were sitting around waiting for further instructions. Coming out of my stupor, I realized that the corporal was calling my name. I had never heard my name called out like this. One of the things I learned that day was that my name was to be changed again. Now it was "Smith, John P."

The corporal said, "The sergeant wants to see you. Follow me." Without comment, I picked up my small bag of personal belongings and followed the corporal through the hundreds of men who sat about. At the far end of the depot, the sergeant sat in his office. He was dressed in his green uniform, decorated with many colorful ribbons on his chest; but it was his sergeant stripes, three up and two rockers, that caused me to wonder what kind of sergeant he was, given the number of stripes. His manner was easy and affable, and he was smiling from behind his oversized GI-issue, horn-rimmed glasses.

"I have been waiting for you for five years," he said happily.

"What?" I replied. "Why were you waiting for me?"

"I have been waiting for you for five years and now you are here," the sergeant repeated.

This conversation is going nowhere, I thought to myself, so I remained silent.

The sergeant continued, "Let me explain. I have been in charge of this recruiting station for five years, and you are the first person to pass all of our examinations high enough to qualify for the army's intelligence school, and you are also the required minimum age, 21 years old. Would you like to go to intelligence school?"

"What does that mean?" I asked, with some real concern for the required enlistment time.

"It means I get to fill a slot that I haven't been able to fill for five years, and you get a great deal," he replied. "As a counterintelligence agent, you will not have to wear a uniform, and you will get to investigate people. The job is like the army's FBI. You also scored the highest score I have ever seen on a language aptitude test, and I also can send you to language school." Latin and Spanish helped there, I thought to myself.

The sergeant really got my attention when he said, "Once we're done with all of your training, there will be barely time for you to go to Vietnam, and if you study French or German, you are likely to end up in Europe."

I asked what was required of me.

"Well, you will need to sign up for four years."

I immediately became suspicious and said, "I will do the two-year draft and out."

The sergeant turned serious and said, "You will go to Vietnam and be killed. The draft is for the infantry, cannon fodder. That's where all of these boys are going. You really don't want to do that. I'm doing you a favor. Give me three years, not the four, and I'll guarantee, after basic training you will go to intelligence school and language school. That will take up the first two years of your enlistment. Vietnam will be over."

I asked him for a few minutes to think about it, and he said, "Go have lunch on me and see me when you get back." He gave me a government food voucher and a list of the nearby restaurants that would accept the voucher. I gathered myself, walked out of the depot dazed and found a nearby coffee shop that was on his list.

I ordered the blue plate special - roast beef, mashed potatoes and gravy with a dinner roll. I also had a Coke which put me over the five dollar value of the voucher by seven cents.

There was no one to talk to about this decision. I was somewhat depressed because of my departure from Gethsemani, believing I had failed myself and God. I had nowhere to go and no idea of what I wanted to do. I had no job, no money, no friends, few relatives and, it seemed - no choices. I would have to trust the sergeant and take his offer.

Walking back toward the depot in a cold light rain only depressed me further and I felt trapped. Even God was silent because we weren't on speaking terms just then. I was alone, and I alone would become a soldier.

The sergeant greeted me in the same manner as before, good-naturedly. After I signed the enlistment papers, he sent me off to rejoin the masses waiting in the depot.

"Do me proud," he said. I left silently, not able to even smile or say thank you.

Then it began, the induction - long lines for shots, lectures and schedules. Then we were sent to dinner with another voucher and ordered to be back by 7 p.m. to board buses for Fort Benning, Georgia. Everything moved efficiently, but there was a tension in the air so palpable I felt sick.

We boarded the buses. Exuberant youth talked endlessly through the night about how they were going to kill "gooks" and win medals. Most talked about "jump school" and how only the hardest of men would finish the training to become paratroopers or

Special Forces.

I was four years older than all of the others, and felt that I had absolutely nothing in common with them, save being a young boy in Appalachia. I said little. I did not want to be a paratrooper or kill anyone.

The ride seemed endless but finally sometime around 4 a.m., we arrived at Ft. Benning. The buses began to break off from our caravan and move to various groupings of barracks and other buildings. I knew from every war movie I had seen that we were about to arrive at Basic Training.

As I peered through the bus window into the haze of the night, our driver pulled into an open area in front of a row of old barracks. Four or five other buses followed. I recognized a cadre of drill instructors (DI) from their unique headgear, the Smokey Bear hat. They were waiting, hands on their hips, looking expectantly at the buses as we arrived. The DIs seemed to be snarling, ready to do battle.

The door of our bus opened, startling me, and a drill sergeant, his Smokey Bear cocked on the bridge of his nose, and a lighted cigar stuffed in his mouth, greeted us loudly, "Good morning, girls. I'm your DI, your new mommy and daddy, Sergeant Smith. Get your asses off this bus right now." Could this be real, I wondered: Sergeant Smith?

The ensuing chaos was hysterical but no one was laughing, and orders were being barked for us to line up in some manner that made absolutely no sense to me at the time. The DIs were yelling, pushing and shoving to get the lines adjusted so that we could "stand tall," as we were told. I ended up in the front line of the haphazard formation. Now in four platoons we would form a new company of trainees, numbering about 250.

Sergeant Smith barked us to attention and the company commander stepped forward. I assessed him to be a young captain. His welcome was brief, sprinkled with patriotism, calls to duty and, ironically, how worthless we were as civilians but how great we would be in a short eight weeks. He finished his speech and turned us over to the DIs.

Sergeant Smith stepped to the front of what was now our platoon and asked if anyone could type. One young man stepped forward, and Sergeant Smith said to him, "You are now the company clerk," whatever that meant.

Then he asked, "Who has graduated from college?" No one said anything or stepped forward.

"Does anyone have some college?"

I said, "Yes, sir," and stepped forward. Sergeant Smith placed himself directly in front of me, with his burning cigar nearly on the end of my nose, and asked my name.

"Perry Smith," I said.

"That is not your name. What is your name?"

"John Smith."

"That is not your name, you fucking idiot. You see, men, that's the problem with these college boys, they really don't know anything. Your name, Soldier, is Smith, John P., and it is to my great regret that our last names are the same. You are about to have the worst eight weeks of your life."

And so they were. I pulled extra guard duty, long hours of kitchen duty (KP) and was generally harassed most of the time, getting extra push-ups and lots of time running about with an M-14 rifle held over my head with both hands.

But then, in week six, something very odd happened. Sergeant Smith called me to the company office and said, "Who do you know? Who is your daddy? Are you some kind of senator's kid or what?"

I was completely baffled and had no idea what he was talking about. When I denied being connected to anyone of importance, he said, "Well, you damn well know somebody, because you are the only son of a bitch in this entire brigade who has gotten orders to go to Fort Holabird, the U.S. Army's intelligence school. Not only that, you have continuing orders to go to the Defense Language Institute (DLI) in California, after Fort Holabird. So who the hell do you know?"

I remained stoic and simply said, "A sergeant in Ashland, Kentucky."

Smith ordered me out of his office. I overheard him tell the clerk, "That bastard's lying. His daddy is connected somewhere."

The harassment and extra duty stopped.

As it turned out, all of the promises the sergeant in Ashland made to me came true, with the exception of not making a trip to Vietnam. Nonetheless, little did I know at the time that this gregarious Army recruiter set me on a path that would change my life completely and give me the beginning of a profession that would ultimately last nearly 35 years.

Ft. Holabird, Baltimore, Maryland

Intelligence training at Ft. Holabird was as much fun as anyone could possibly have while in the army. The classes in photography, wire tapping, surveillance, counter- surveillance, interviewing and interrogation were stimulating and practical, and as far as any of us knew, directly applicable to the work we would be doing in our future assignments.

Soon after getting acclimated to Ft. Holabird, I contacted my cousin, another John Smith, in nearby Arlington, Virginia. We knew each other fairly well and were close in age. Soon we were "out on the town" in Washington on several successive weekends. John and I met his old friend from Florida, Ellen, and her three roommates. The three others were from Pittsburgh and had made their way to Washington. All were working as clerk typists at the FBI. After a false start with Linda, a funny and fun-loving sort, Penny Orman and I were smitten. I spent every available moment with her.

Penny invited me to her family home for what was to become our first Christmas together. Her mother immediately recognized the seriousness of our relationship and was deeply concerned we had gotten too serious in too short a time. I think she was glad that once I finished training at Ft. Holabird, I would move on to Monterey, California, for language school.

Graduation from Ft. Holabird was a low-key affair and my orders were to report immediately to Defense Language Institute at Monterey to start the new cycle of classes in October 1966. Allegedly, French would enable me to talk to the Vietnamese. Orders to Vietnam had also been included with the assignment to DLI. My Ashland sergeant had been wrong about Vietnam unless the war ended in six months. Nonetheless, I was happy to study French in the amazingly beautiful Monterey Bay setting.

9th Infantry Division, Bear Cat, Viet Nam

In April 1967 I arrived in Vietnam and was assigned to a staff job at U.S. Army Headquarters Vietnam, Saigon. After numerous requests to be assigned to combat operations, I was finally assigned in December 1967 to the 9th Military Intelligence Detachment at Bear Cat, the 9th Infantry's division headquarters. Much of our work was conducted up and down Highway 4 attempting to determine how the Viet Cong were anticipating our tactical operations or where they might strike us next. Our mission was really to thwart Viet Cong intelligence operations against the 9th Infantry. Reliable Vietnamese sources or informants in the outlying villages were key to our success.

Our bases were deeply compromised by Viet Cong intelligence collection efforts. It was easy for them to elicit or coerce information from the Vietnamese nationals who worked on practically every U.S. military facility in Vietnam. Their effectiveness showed in many successful Viet Cong attacks on facilities and convoys.

The 11th Armored Cavalry Regiment, in support of 9th Infantry operations, had carved out a base camp in a dense jungle along Interprovincial Highway 2, twelve kilometers south of Xuan Loc. It was known as Blackhorse Camp. The 11th Cavalry provided convoy escort and clearing operations when and where called upon.

In late December, a column of sixteen armored vehicles of the 11th Cavalry moved south along the Xuan Loc/Vung Tau Highway and were ambushed in the middle of the jungle. The lead tank and the last vehicle in the column were hit first, and then methodically every vehicle in between was hit by armor-piercing grenades. From their dug-in positions scant yards from the highway, the Viet Cong successfully took out an entire armored column in less than five minutes. They broke off immediately and ran into the jungle.

Most of our troops were killed with only two or three surviving the assault.

General Creighton Abrams, of World War II fame as an armored cavalry commander, was outraged and was calling for a full explanation and accounting. I was assigned to investigate the incident to determine how this could have happened.

As I flew by helicopter to Blackhorse Camp to interview anyone and everyone who had anything to do with this column's move to Vung Tau, I realized that no matter how this investigation turned out, there would be severe consequences.

It was clear that the Viet Cong knew precisely the date, time and size of the column. They were waiting and, with terrible efficiency, killed almost everyone.

The investigation determined that the troops involved in the move to Vung Tau had known for some weeks that they were being moved. There was talk all over the camp. Some troops had even made arrangements with their Vietnamese girlfriends and camp support personnel to follow them to Vung Tau.

There was a lot of radio communication between Blackhorse and Vung Tau openly talking about the transfer. There were written communications, with little or no control of access. I also learned that earlier sweep operations along the highway between Blackhorse and Vung Tau had discovered rudimentary wiretap intercept equipment used by the Viet Cong.

As the senior investigator, I concluded that this terrible tragedy occurred because the troops had compromised the movement of their column by openly talking about it to the many Vietnamese working at Blackhorse Camp. It had been the buzz for at least two weeks prior to that fateful day. Further, I did not consider it out of the realm of possibility that the Viet Cong had the capability to intercept our wire communications.

My briefing to General Abrams and his staff was short and to the point. I thought we all were to blame for completely underestimating the intelligence collection capability of the Viet Cong. He was tremendously angry but had nowhere to put his anger and no one to blame. The commanding officer for this armored column had been killed in the assault.

Dong Tam

In mid-January 1968 I was assigned as the senior counterintelligence agent at the 9th Military Intelligence Detachment, 2nd Brigade (Riverine) at Dong Tam, some seven kilometers west of the provincial capital of My Tho.

When I arrived there, I found the seven-man unit to be completely demoralized, having taken a number of severe casualties in the previous six months. They also lacked a clear understanding of their mission and had suffered weak leadership from the time they established the detachment at Dong Tam.

The detachment was housed on the bottom floor of a two-story barracks-like structure, made of pinewood and screens. The 9th Military Police was billeted on the top floor.

Viet Cong activity in the province was relentless and their frequent mortar attacks left us vulnerable. Our task was to recruit informants among the Vietnamese and the troops to determine how the Viet Cong were collecting information on us and what they knew. This was no easy task. The detachment had a few sources and needed to be more aggressive in developing information and informants in the nearby villages and in My Tho. Most of our Vietnamese workers came from these villages.

Dong Tam was an approximately 900-acre sand pile dug out of the Mekong River itself. It was a major operational base for the 2nd Brigade (Riverine) with a myriad of tactical air and river units as well as a host of support units. The immediate problem, from a counterintelligence perspective, was that many South Vietnamese nationals worked on the base.

Present in almost every activity on the base, the Vietnamese did everything from shining shoes to laundry to cooking and working in the post exchange. Base security and the Vietnamese National Police had allegedly cleared all of them. In truth, this was a farce. Our vulnerability was extreme.

Because of the earlier casualties the unit had suffered I immediately set out to build a bunker large enough to protect the detachment and the MPs during mortar and rocket attacks. Some made fun of this effort, thinking it silly, but as it turned out, it saved a number of us during the increasing number of mortar attacks that led up to and continued during Tet 1968.

My daily routine involved going to the morning briefings in

the Tactical Operations Center (TOC), coordinating tactical intel requirements with the brigade's senior intelligence officer and taking
orders from the on-base commanding officer to support any field
operations about to be undertaken. I was also responsible for intelligence sharing and coordination with the CIA based in My Tho, and
the Navy's Special Operations (SEAL) team assigned at Dong Tam.

The 1968 Tet Offensive

Tet 1968 took a terrible toll on the 9th Division, beginning with
an assault on a forward artillery battery camped out in the middle of
the jungle just north of Dong Tam. Word came to me at about 1:30
in the morning that I should come to the TOC immediately. On my
arrival, I learned that the artillery unit may have been wiped out by
a Viet Cong assault. Communications had stopped during the battle.
At first light, several of us were airlifted to the unit's position. Their
battery had been completely overrun, the perimeter on all sides was
compromised, and hand-to-hand combat had occurred.

There was strong physical evidence to suggest that the Viet
Cong had for some days been digging positions around the battery
and had penetrated the perimeter after the troops had fallen asleep.
The perimeter had been secured only marginally with concertina
wire and some claymore mines for protection. The Viet Cong had
cut through the wire, gone into the camp, closed the doors of the
track vehicles with troops sleeping in them, and secured the closed
doors with wire.

The noise from closing those doors should have awakened the
troops, but they had been drinking earlier in the evening. The Viet
Cong then backed off and fired armor piercing grenades into their

targets, incinerating the soldiers.

The few survivors were severely injured. Only a few blood trails of the Viet Cong wounded were found as they retreated into the jungle. We concluded that they had few casualties. Our troops had been taken by surprise and slaughtered.

As things deteriorated in and around Saigon during Tet, the 2nd Brigade moved to help defend Saigon. Those of us that remained behind were more vulnerable at Dong Tam than we had ever been and we were constantly harassed by mortar and small-arms fire on our perimeter. Surprisingly, no major attempt was made to overrun the base.

Instead a main force VC Battalion viciously attacked My Tho, killing several thousand civilians and South Vietnamese soldiers. Much of the nine days of fighting there occurred around the National Police and CIA compounds. Much to the credit of the valor of some of the National Police, their American advisors and a company of South Vietnamese marines, that sector of the city successfully resisted being taken.

On the other hand, there were many accounts of the South Vietnamese army breaking and running. There was an occasion during the Tet offensive when they left their U.S. military advisors to absorb the assault of the oncoming Viet Cong at the My Tho Bridge.

Out of the battle of My Tho, Viet Cong documents were found, one of which affected me. It was a Viet Cong hit list for a number of U.S. officers and key personnel at Dong Tam and My Tho. The accuracy of this list was spot on, with name, rank, serial number and unit identification spelled out precisely.

My name was on the list and identified me as an intelligence officer. Another fifteen or so were identified similarly. This information could have come only from the personnel files on the base or from our personal association with Vietnamese counterparts and/or girlfriends. Our investigation was inconclusive with respect to the personnel files because most were kept at division headquarters. No Vietnamese workers seemed to have direct access to the scant files at Dong Tam.

I had been seeing for some months a beautiful, young Vietnamese widow who had an infant son. Her South Vietnamese soldier husband had been killed before their son was born. She lived in My Tho proper. I had been to her home several times for meals and family get-togethers. A few days after learning about this list, I confronted her, demanding that she explain why the Viet Cong knew my name and about my unit. I was fairly certain she had seen my dog tags but she did not know about my intelligence affiliation, at least not from me.

Initially, she denied knowing anything but when I threatened her, pushing her hard up against the wall, she began to explain.

She said, "Of course I know the Viet Cong. They killed my husband. We all grew up together in this neighborhood. And they control everything that happens here. Why do you think you are alive?" she asked.

Answering her own question, she said, "They could have killed you anytime you visited here, but they didn't because I told them who you were, and they also knew you were helping me with my baby. Yes, I told them about you to protect you, my baby and me. If I had not, they would have killed us all."

After I calmed down, we talked about how all this affected us and what it meant for her future. She said, "I am not treated well by many Vietnamese because I have associated with you and I work at Dong Tam. Most Vietnamese only want peace. We want to be able to have our children, make a home, work and have enough to eat; beyond that, most of us do not expect much more."

She went on to say, "It really doesn't make much difference whether we are governed by Ho Chi Minh or by the United States government. Politics and war are for the rich. I hope only to survive and see my son grow up."

There was nothing more to be said or to be done. I left her, sadly reminded of my own failure to protect the others for whom I was responsible, and for stupidly putting myself at risk. Yet I was grateful that this kind and practical woman had saved my life.

*****

The assistant division commander of the 9th Infantry Division, Brigadier General William A. Knowlton, like every good senior officer, was rightly concerned about troop morale and esprit de corps. So he began to spend more and more time at Dong Tam instead of being ferried back and forth between division headquarters and the 2nd Brigade. He was given an ample two-bedroom trailer and the appropriate furnishings commensurate with his rank.

Viet Cong activity around Dong Tam continued at a steady pace, with the usual frequent night mortar attacks. Often the Viet Cong preferred to mortar our base from the courtyard of a Buddhist pagoda in Tan Phu, a small village very near our perimeter.

At that time, this pagoda, like all other religious structures or sites in Vietnam, could not be fired upon, as a matter of political and military policy. The harassment from this particular Viet Cong position was irritating everyone up and down the chain of command. We were able to triangulate exactly their position for an easy kill, but we had to let them continue lobbing shells into the base.

The troops looked forward to their mail, time out from the field, Rest and Relaxation (R&R) to exotic places and drinking beer. One afternoon a Chinook helicopter had airlifted an enormous pallet of beer onto the base and put it under a tent. That night, Viet Cong, from their privileged position in the pagoda, lobbed a number of rounds into our compound, two rounds hitting the newly arrived beer supply and the chapel, and another hitting the general's new trailer.

During the morning briefing, General Knowlton was upset, but not about his quarters being hit. He was concerned about the troops, losing both the beer and the chapel in a single attack, coming from a location we could not fire upon.

"Not good for troop morale," the general said. He asked me what I could do to stop this harassment from the pagoda without actually attacking or damaging the pagoda. I assured him that I would immediately talk to my counterparts in the CIA and the SEAL team and devise a plan to stop these attacks. I spoke with other team members and we decided to do a nighttime insertion of a five- or six-man team to capture or kill the Viet Cong as they made their way to the pagoda. This would require undetected entry into the jungle by the team.

As a cover to collect information about how we could easily access the pagoda we ran a sweep or two through the village, searching for weapons. The sweeps produced one cache of weapons and a small firefight, killing a seven-man Viet Cong squad. The good news was that we found the paths through the jungle that were allowing the Viet Cong to slip in and out of the village and the pagoda. We inserted a seven-man team under the cover of night, and they lay in the jungle awaiting the mortar unit.

It was as if the Viet Cong had vanished. There was no attack from the pagoda for two weeks. We stopped the operation but, on the very night we were not waiting, another attack came from the pagoda.

The next morning, General Knowlton told me, "This Viet Cong unit is raising hell with us, and I want it stopped now. Do whatever you have to do."

We reinserted a smaller team, believing it would be less noticeable but, again, no Viet Cong came to the pagoda. It was clear to me that there was a security problem, that the leak could have come from anywhere on the base, to include my own unit interpreters, who were Vietnamese.

The SEAL team leader, CIA chief and I decided to publicly stand-down the operation but clandestinely send in a team consisting only of SEALs. They had to wait only two days before the Viet Cong mortar squad came walking through our trap on the way to the pagoda. Four were killed and three taken prisoner.

Riding on the River

Early one morning, Captain John Hasemen, 9th MID commanding officer (forward), and I, with our interpreter, loaded the three handcuffed Viet Cong onto a small boat and proceeded from our base camp, Dong Tam, to the Navy fast-boat station in My Tho; we were some six to eight kilometers away. The Mekong River was tidal with six- to eight-foot swells at times, and the tide was coming in strongly as we left the base.

As I navigated the boat toward the middle of the river and we settled in for the ride, Haseman commented, as we looked to our right at Thoi Son Island, "What a great place for an ambush."

He had no more said the words when we started receiving small arms and automatic-weapons fire from a tree line on the shore. In my haste to get us out of range, I had forgotten that the throttle had been shortened in a repair and forward was now reverse.

As I pushed down hard, I stalled the engine. We were sitting ducks and floating like a cork in the river. I ordered everyone out of the boat to the left side, to give them cover, and the five jumped overboard. The interpreter and Haseman hung onto the prisoners, keeping them from drowning.

I remained in the boat, stretched out behind the motor, trying to adjust the air-fuel intake so I could restart the motor. As I stretched out over the back of the boat working on the motor, a burst of AK-47 fire hit the water near the motor and my helmet, sending it flying into the river.

I was stunned but not hit, and I continued to fiddle with the carburetor. In a few more moments, I had the engine started, and I turned hard left in the opposite direction of the gunfire. My five passengers hung onto the side of the boat as we moved quickly out of rangle. The gunfire stopped and we somehow managed to get everybody back into the boat.

A short time later, as we arrived at the Navy facility, I began
to pull in toward the dock, which was made of iron and concrete
and designed for much larger boats. We were some ten feet below
the top of the dock. The tide was swirling in and around the dock,
making our docking a little tricky. I looked up and noticed the South
Vietnamese National Police and several U.S. Navy officers awaiting
our arrival, as had been planned.

In my distraction, we were caught in a tremendous swirl, being pulled rapidly toward the dock. I panicked and again pulled the
throttle in the wrong direction, now sending us hurtling toward the
dock, crashing into it with an awful force.

The three prisoners went overboard, and Haseman and our interpreter struggled to hold onto them, as people on the dock threw
lines to our rescue. The front of the boat was badly damaged and
taking on water. The officers on the dock and I secured the boat
to stop it from completely sinking, and finally I climbed up on the
dock.

The naval officers were now laughing hysterically. They saluted and the senior officer greeted me, "Splendid job coming alongside, Admiral Perry."

In spite of the fact I had nearly killed all of us, it was funny.
Things settled down and the Viet Cong prisoners were handed over
to the national police. Our interpreter went into the city to see his
wife. Haseman and I were invited to the mess for something to drink
and eat.

As we sat at the table and recounted the morning's events, I
began to shake uncontrollably. Panicked, I thought I was having
a nervous breakdown. A medic was called, and he took my blood

pressure and pronounced it was high, but said I should be all right as soon as I got over the shock of what had happened.

I kept repeating in my head: "You are an idiot! You have only 13 days left in country and you're going to get killed." I kept thinking how stupid I was to have rejected CI Section Chief Captain Erickson's offer to bring me out of the field. Two weeks earlier, he had called from division headquarters saying that I was thirty days from going home, and he felt that, given the level of combat in our area of operations, I should come back to headquarters for the remainder of my time in country.

The navy hoisted the damaged boat onto the back of a deuce-and-a-half truck, and we drove back to Dong Tam. Once arriving at our compound, we offloaded the boat next to the office and settled in. I called Erickson at Division and asked if the offer to come to Bear Cat was still open. He said it was. He instructed me to take two days to close out my affairs at Dong Tam and report to Division.

A routine helicopter flight that ferried between division headquarters and Dong Tam was my ticket out on the third morning. As I boarded the aircraft, the pilot said, "I understand you're on your way home. We'll make sure to get you there, since you're so 'short.' " I'm going to fly this thing as high as it will go."

My ten days at headquarters were filled with anticipation as to my next assignment since my orders had not arrived. There was no going home without orders. A clerk in the assignment management office queried Washington. Two days later the clerk notified me that a reply had come and I should come to see his lieutenant.

As I stood waiting to be acknowledged by the lieutenant seated behind his desk, he asked, "Whom do you know?" I asked what he meant. "Your orders came directly from the Secretary of the Army. Whom do you know?"

Amused, I said, "A sergeant in Ashland, Kentucky."

The lieutenant was not amused and commented, "I have never seen orders cut directly from the Secretary of the Army's office. You have to know someone or be the son of a general to get this kind of attention." I stuck to my story.

Only after returning to the States, did I learn that Penny had asked my Aunt Mayme, who was a secretary at the Pentagon in the Secretary of the Army's office, to see if I could somehow be reassigned to the 116th Military Intelligence Group in Washington, D.C. Aunt Mayme quietly intervened.

One Man's View

From a counterintelligence perspective, I believe we greatly underestimated our enemy on many levels but particularly with respect to Viet Cong intelligence-collection skills. It is true, they were not very sophisticated, but they were effective and there is no doubt that our bases were penetrated top to bottom by Viet Cong sources.

There is also no doubt that we foolishly consorted with the South Vietnamese as if we were confident that they could be trusted. There were many that we trusted with our lives and many deserved that trust and died for us; however, we often lost sight of the fundamental truths that ruled daily life in Vietnam. My girlfriend was a case in point. She wanted only peace and to have a good life, but she was driven to survive and thus did what she did.

When we were preparing the Blackhorse Camp incident report,

several officers thought that the idea that the Viet Cong could con-duct voice intercept of our communications was laughable. Several of them said that they had never met a Vietnamese who could speak or understand English well. As ludicrous as this assertion was, there was a prejudice among us that gave us confidence to talk openly in the hearing of the Vietnamese, thinking we were not understood. We were overly trusting and I believe it was fatal in some cases. I know it certainly was fatal in the case of Blackhorse.

While I would not presume to speak for anyone else or out-side of my own narrow experience in Vietnam, I know that intelli-gence failures were at the root of many of the operational disasters. We simply could not, with any accuracy or confidence, anticipate what the Viet Cong were up to or what they would do next. Our base camps leaked like sieves because we were open and friendly to those we trusted, and the enemy was listening.

Going Home

On my one-year anniversary date of arriving in Vietnam, I left on a chartered evening flight bound for Hawaii, then Anchorage and then on to Dover Air Force Base in Delaware. Hours after arriving in Delaware, I caught a commercial flight to Washington, D.C., where Penny, the woman I would marry, was waiting.

Penny and I spent days and weeks getting reacquainted. I moved into my aunt's home as a paying boarder, bought a car and shopped for new clothes. My authorized three weeks' leave went by quickly. This was a wonderful time for Penny and me, yet I was hav-ing some troubling nightmares about Vietnam, and I found myself breaking into a sweat and shaking when we crossed any bridge. I had been nearly killed in an incident near Dong Tam when the Viet Cong blew up a bridge as we passed over it in our jeep. I had no idea how profoundly affected I had been by this event until I got back to the States.

Arlington, Virginia, is situated across the Potomac River from Washington, and I was soon to be crossing the Fourteenth Street Bridge every workday to get to my new unit at Fort McNair. I knew I was in trouble and I somehow fell upon the idea of trying what is known in psychology as implosion therapy. This was an intuitive choice, knowing only that, if I was afraid of something, I had to repeat the act that caused the fear until such time as the fear subsided or went away. Fighting bulls had taught me that.

The Sunday before I was to report to the 116th MI Group, Penny and I got into my brand-new 1968 green Ford Mustang and repeatedly drove back and forth across the Fourteenth Street Bridge for about five hours. She drove the first hour or so until I became somewhat comfortable and then I took the wheel. The implosion therapy worked, enabling me to report to work.

Penny and I married in December 1968. She worked for Westinghouse Electric Corporation on K Street. I got an early out from the army to start school at The George Washington University. The GI Bill combined with her income enabled me to finish in two years a Bachelor of Arts degree in international affairs with a specialization in Latin American studies. Then in June 1971, we began our career with the CIA.

Memorial Days

In the years following my return from Vietnam, I avoided any

Memorial Day service or news accounts of them. I also steadfastly refused to visit the Vietnam War Memorial once it was completed. My best friend, Jon Thomas, also a veteran of Vietnam, had frequently visited The Wall, as the memorial had been dubbed. He often encouraged me to make a visit, but I could not. Penny also encouraged me to visit The Wall, to seek some personal closure and peace about Vietnam, but I refused.

Years later, another especially important Memorial Day was approaching and I was making plans to get out of Washington to avoid the usual parade and services. It was May 28, 1984, when the internment took place of the Unknown Solider lost in Vietnam. Our plans fell through and Penny arranged for us to get together with Jon and his wife, Susan, in the afternoon for a picnic.

After breakfast, Penny gently said that she wanted to go to the Memorial Day parade in Washington. She suggested that we go to the Lincoln Memorial and watch the parade from there. My immediate response was, "No."

She answered kindly, "Perry you need to go. You must make peace with Vietnam. Please take me, and I will be there with you."

Little was said as we made our way into Washington and navigated the growing traffic and crowd. We were able to find a place on the Lincoln Memorial circle as it exits onto the Memorial Bridge in the direction of Arlington Cemetery. Standing near the edge of the sidewalk with only a few people around us, we had a close and clear view.

My memory of that day is still a blur, recalling only that Penny held my left hand, and I saluted the flags, troops, and finally the army caisson carrying the remains, accompanied by the black, riderless horse as they passed in front of us. Tears poured down my cheeks as I wept uncontrollably.

We spent the afternoon as planned with Jon and Susan and our children. Penny mentioned that we had gone to the parade, but I said nothing. Jon commented that he thought it was good, and he renewed his interest in having me visit the Vietnam War Memorial. I couldn't fathom the idea, given what had happened at the Lincoln Memorial.

I was afraid I would suffer a complete breakdown. I had no real idea of how emotionally damaged I was by the war. I certainly was aware I had not come home as the same person who went to Vietnam but, for me, being wounded in Vietnam meant a physical wound, a blown-off limb or gunshot injury. "Battle fatigue" or "post-traumatic stress syndrome" really meant nothing to me, yet I certainly was symptomatic.

It was another four years before Jon eventually persuaded me to walk over to The Wall. He was then the Assistant Secretary of State for narcotics and I was a supervisor at FBI Headquarters.

Jon somehow knew that I might be ready to visit the memorial. Meeting him at his office at the State Department to discuss a work related matter, Jon suggested we take a walk outside since it was a beautiful spring day.

We were discussing a drug enforcement policy matter when he proposed that we cut through the mall area to continue our walk down by the Potomac. I mockingly told him he was not very clever, trying to trick me into going to The Wall.

He said, "Just walk through with me. We don't have to stop or really think about it. We'll go in on one end and out the other. Don't even look at the names." I nodded and mumbled a grudging, "OK." I followed Jon.

As we walked past the veterans who were helping visitors to look up names of the dead and where they were located on The Wall, I stiffened. But just as he promised, we hit a quick stride and walked to the other end and out.

The beauty of The Wall in its simplicity and stark presentation stunned me. As we continued to walk, I told Jon that I thought it fitting a Vietnamese woman had designed it. Its understated, reverent style appealed to my contemplative nature and preference for clean linear design. I thought it Trappist like.

Over the years, Jon and I have visited The Wall several times together. Each visit has been more healing but they have always been emotionally unpredictable. There is no rhyme nor reason to how I am moved at the time of my visits. I make no special effort these days to visit The Wall when I am in Washington. Yet each time I am there, I find some new hope that allows me to believe that in God's greatness and mercy we will somehow be forgiven our precious losses and the terrible things we did.

Vietnam, 1968

Houng, 1968, Dong Tam, Vietnam

Houng and her son, 1968, My Tho, South Vietnam

8 ✠

The Search Begins

Shortly after mother's death, I again questioned Aunt Alma about the details of my adoption. She was more reticent than ever, and offered nothing new. I was certain that mother had instructed her, either shortly before or maybe on the day that she died, to keep her secret and not reveal anything. It would have been just like Mother to pull rank as the older sister and instruct Aunt Alma to stay quiet.

My next most serious attempt to locate my biological parents came some years later, shortly after I was married. My wife Penny and I were visiting Logan to see Aunt Alma, my brother David and Aunt Tildie. Tildie Ellis was the long time matriarch of the Whitman-Perry side of the family, and was the favorite aunt of my mother. She was in her nineties, but acutely sharp. Now that I was married and having returned from Viet Nam, I thought perhaps Aunt Tildie would talk to me openly.

Aunt Tildie was a plainspoken woman of some local fame. She had been the Clerk of Court for many years and ran the Democratic political machine in Logan County. There are amazing stories about Aunt Tildie, her sense of justice and fair play, and her political connections and hard-nosed commitment to the Democratic Party. Wid-

owed early in her marriage to John, Aunt Tildie never remarried or
had children, but rather chose to dote on her sister's oldest child,
my mother, Yuma. She smoked Kool cigarettes incessantly, wore an
apron as part of her uniform of the day, played a very mean game of
canasta, and loved to hold forth. She taught me to play solitaire and
how to string beans.

There was no more strident, vocal, enthusiastic fan of the Cincinnati Reds than our Aunt Tildie. She was such a part of Logan
County's folklore and history that everyone called her Aunt Tildie,
including Senators Byrd and Stevenson, and her favorite politician,
John F. Kennedy, whom she had met when he came to Logan County to win her support for his presidential bid. She was a formidable
and powerful woman. I liked her very much, and I knew that she
liked me as well, if for no other reason than I was the son of her
favorite niece.

My strategy was simple, to ask her directly what she knew about
my adoption. She confirmed what I had suspected for a long time,
that I was illegitimate. She recalled that my two mothers had been
friends, and there had been significant contact between them, both
prior to and after my adoption in February 1946. She also recalled
that my biological mother was from Kentucky, either the Somerset
or Danville area. Aunt Tildie confirmed what had been told to me
on that Halloween night about mother's destruction of the adoption
papers. She was not able to remember my biological mother's name.

I pressed her for more details as to the age of my biological
mother, and she simply said she did not know. I asked if there was
any possibility that I had been born out of wedlock to a woman that
my father had had a relationship with for many years. Aunt Tildie
knew the story about my father having had a long-term relationship

in Chattanooga, but felt certain that there was no connection between that affair and me. I was pleasantly surprised and energized by this new information, and felt certain that I knew at least part of the story, which would lead to other clues in Somerset or Danville, Kentucky.

For as long as I could remember during the years we lived in Logan, each summer my mother would take David and me to Somerset and Danville to visit friends. We often stayed in Somerset with Jack and Irene Dutton. They had a daughter, Sherry, and I thought that perhaps I might have been Sherry's son. Sherry was shy, pretty, older and living at home at an age when I thought she should have been out on her own.

A few short weeks after visiting Aunt Tildie, I went to Somerset and Danville to try to find Irene Dutton or her husband. Once there, I found them in the telephone book and called their residence. There was no answer so I went to their home. It was a normal workday and I found no one at home, but, through a neighbor, I learned that Irene was working in a fabric store not far from her home. I arrived at the store at about noon, and after a few inquiries, I found Irene. I introduced myself. She warmly embraced me and immediately asked about what had happened in the intervening years. I made some small talk, but almost immediately got to the issue. I must have seemed quite rude since I wanted this information desperately.

When I told her that I thought that perhaps her daughter, Sherry, was my mother, Irene became distressed, and immediately told me it was not true. I told her what Aunt Tildie had said and I pressed pretty hard. Irene convinced me that Sherry was not my mother. She tried to persuade me that Mother had not provided many details about the adoption, but I suspected she had taken a sworn oath that she would never reveal what mother had told her about the adoption. I left the fabric store disheartened and discouraged.

My father's sole surviving brother, Howard Smith, and his wife, Mary, were residents of Somerset as well. That evening I visited them and pressed them hard for details about the adoption. I felt certain that Uncle Howard would have some recollection, given that he was close to my father. He was no help, but was sympathetic to my situation. He confirmed that I was illegitimate and that my mothers had either been friends, or had known each other for some time before the adoption took place. Aunt Mary wanted to help, but strained and struggled with the conversation. I suspected that she knew a lot more than what she was telling, but as in every case, there seemed no way to break through the veil of secrecy.

The next day, the three of us visited my father's gravesite in Danville. As I stood over the marker and watched Aunt Mary arrange some flowers, I desperately wanted my father to be alive. I wanted him to speak to me and tell me the story; I wanted to know the truth. I wanted to know where I had come from and where I belonged.

9 ✠

Spies

Becoming a CIA case officer was a mix and blend of intellectual acumen and the resourcefulness of an actor-warrior. In 1971, we were at the height of the Cold War, with the complication of a bellicose Cuba. The failure of the Bay of Pigs invasion was legend, and many of the CIA officers involved in that attempt to topple Fidel Castro were still active in the agency.

Working in my Cuban uncle's medical office in East Los Angeles where Cuban exiles came every day to see him, I had learned much about Cuba and Cubans. My Spanish was salted with the Cuban accent and colloquial expressions. I loved the Cuban people, and all this made me the perfect candidate to work against them.

There was little doubt as we finished our first year of schooling as career trainees (CTs) that I would be selected to serve in the Latin American Division. Mexico, for example, had never broken diplomatic relations with Cuba and the Cubans had a very large embassy there.

Mexico

In the 1970s, Penny and I were sent to Mexico in a Non-official

Cover (NOC) capacity. This was a wonderful homecoming for me, enabling us to build upon my old friendships from my bullfighting days. We hit the ground running and found a home near my daytime workplace. It was imperative to live fully into the cover job, appearing legitimate at all times. My spy work was to be done at night. The hours were long but tremendously rewarding as well as fun.

Many of my contacts could not have overt relationships with North Americans, necessitating my use of disguises and counter-surveillance techniques to get to these meetings safely. Disguises often took up to two hours a day to prepare. Sometimes I would simply apply a false mustache or beard, darken my hair or use a wig to alter my appearance. Penny would help with the disguises and often would drive me to a drop off place so I could take public transportation.

One safe house for meetings was near the National University, a hotbed of leftist students and anti-gringo sentiment. When going there I had to use a more elaborate and complicated disguise that transformed me into an elderly, crippled Mexican, allowing me to move about in that area without drawing attention to myself. Using public transportation allowed me to "dust-off" any hostile surveillance by changing directions and crossing back over my original routes to check for unusual interest in me and what I was doing. Things went well.

Two incidents, unrelated to my spy work, did happen which caused us to move from Naulcalpan to another neighborhood. The first was that a young Mexican man took an unhealthy interest in my wife and began to stalk her when she left our home mid-mornings to go to language school. As she walked to the bus stop, he would attempt to talk to her from his car as he slowly drove alongside the sidewalk. Although Penny did not understand much of what he was saying, he seemed to be interested in her because she was noticeably pregnant. Once I found out about this, I ambushed him one morning and used a golf club to break his windshield and chase him off.

The second incident was the robbery of our home by our gardener and his son one Sunday afternoon while we were out for lunch. We returned home to find them still in the house, but once they realized we had come home, they made their escape over the backyard wall, as we watched them scamper away. They had emptied out the refrigerator and the pantries, and taken all of our jewelry and some cash from the bedroom.

Penny was more than distraught and pressed me to find a safer place for us to live. We were truly fortunate to eventually move into a lovely, Spanish colonial style duplex in the upper reaches of Chapultepec. There were many foreign diplomats and high ranking Mexican government officials in the neighborhood, so security was better.

On November 16, 1974, our daughter Amy was born at the British-American Hospital in Mexico City. We were extremely excited and happy and celebrated with our friends. During the same period my work situation changed and my contacts in Mexico City recommended a different cover. My working papers had not yet expired, so we had some cushion for planning, and operations continued.

Former CIA officer and defector Philip Agee, in concert with Cuban Intelligence, had begun a series of public exposes of CIA officers assigned throughout Latin America and in some parts of Europe. Agee simply would examine the rosters of U.S. personnel living and working abroad and then, based on the various assignments of those personnel, he would deduce or, from memory, identify who was CIA.

This information would then be provided to the press and, of course, the local press was more than interested in exposing CIA operatives in their country. Agee himself had been assigned to Mexico City early in his career and knew many of the officers still there. When the exposure of the Mexico City station came it was a big story, running for several days, terribly damaging U.S. interests. Fortunately, my cover was such that Agee did not yet know me. I felt fortunate to be an NOC operative, away from the glare of an official assignment.

*****

The time came for me to renew my working papers and my visa status in Mexico. I was not required to travel out of the country, so I went to the appropriate authorities in Mexico City to apply for a new visa. When I appeared to make my request, I was referred to another office adjacent to the main reception area. I was greeted by a military officer, who escorted me into a back office occupied by a military intelligence captain. The escorting officer handed the captain a large, thick file, which turned out to be a hard-copy file of my history in Mexico.

The room was dark and foreboding, and the captain sat behind a small desk. I could see his uniform was starched and well-pressed. Brass on his collar glimmered in the shadows and half light. Sitting almost at attention as he looked at me, I looked back hard to see if I could discern what was on his mind.

I fixed on his oversized "frito bandido" mustache. But this man was no movie caricature of an unfriendly Mexican official; he was lean, intense and all business. In a rather menacing tone, he asked me when I had first come to Mexico. Misunderstanding, I thought he meant during the current period, but he asked again, stressing that he wanted to know the very first time I ever stepped foot into Mexico. I told him it was some years ago, when I had first come to Mexico to fight bulls.

He opened the file in front of him and said, "Yes. That is correct. I have your first tourist visa here. Would you like to see it?"

I demurred, telling him that I was sure it was in the file. Then he asked, "Why did you leave Mexico in 1964?" I told him I went back to California for my mother's funeral.

"When did you return?" he asked.

I said, "A month or two later."

Again, he said, "Correct. I have your paperwork here. Would you like to see it?"

I told him no. I was now very alarmed, realizing that the thick file before him was much more than a series of visas and routine paperwork. I struggled to stay relaxed and keep my composure.

The captain then surprised me completely by showing me a copy of my daughter's birth certificate.

He said, "You understand that your daughter is a Mexican, and our government could make things very hard for you."

I asked him to explain his meaning.

"Mr. Smith, what are you doing in Mexico?"

I replied, "I am working."

He said, "You are not. You have not worked for several months."

Then I realized that I had been under surveillance and I was now fearful of being arrested.

The captain asked, "How did you manage to pay almost $8,000 in cash to the hospital for your daughter's birth?"

"From my savings," I replied.

He said, "That's very odd, because your bank account does not show that you wrote any check for that amount of money, so where did you get the money?"

I glibly replied that I had it stuffed in my mattress. The captain was not amused and reminded me that I could be arrested for lying to a government official. I was now completely panicked and convinced I would be in custody shortly.

I explained to the captain that I wanted only to continue living in Mexico; I simply needed a visa.

"Mr. Smith, we have no idea what you are doing in our country. I suspect you are a drug dealer or perhaps a money-launderer or perhaps a pimp or maybe even a spy. We really don't know. What I do know is that you are no longer welcome in Mexico, and you have fourteen days to leave the country. If you do not comply with this order, you and your family will be arrested and escorted from the country as undesirables. You will never be able to return to Mexico."

Before I could answer or protest, he said, "You may leave."

As I made my way out to the street, I was anxious about what the Mexican authorities really knew, what part of my operations might have been compromised, and how to comply with his order. I spent two hours "dusting off," running counter-surveillance patterns on and off public transportation to ensure I was not being followed. I eventually made my way to the popular tourist spot, Sanborn's restaurant, and called my contact in Mexico City activating an emergency meeting.

We met two hours later at a prearranged point, and I described my meeting with the captain. My contact agreed that the boss would want to meet with me as soon as possible to discuss how best to leave the country. The obvious concern was for my sources and handing them over securely to another case officer.

The chief was reassuring and felt that little or no damage had been done or the Mexican government would have made an example of me in public by either arresting me or deporting me as a spy. He believed, as I did, that the captain told the truth when he said that they were not sure about my activities, but had decided in favor of throwing me out of the country.

The chief authorized me to leave Mexico, a people and country that had given me so much. It was a love lost now and I was forced to leave. Penny and Amy left the country almost immediately, and I followed about eight days later, once I had closed out my work there and said goodbye to friends.

*****

Penny and Amy went to Pittsburgh to spend some time with family. I returned to Washington and reported in to CIA headquarters at Langley. I decided to take a couple of weeks of leave to look for a house.

After a few days, Penny joined me and we began our search for a new home in Northern Virginia in anticipation of being assigned to Langley. We found a quaint, small colonial-style house. The house required some repairs but nothing that I could not accomplish by myself with the help of a contractor friend. Once the house was purchased, we began repairs, and Penny returned to Pittsburgh to be with her mother. I went to work at CIA headquarters in the Latin American Division.

The former Mexico City boss was now the chief of the Latin American Division. I hoped for a senior assignment in the division because of my good relationship with him and having just worked for him in Mexico City.

One afternoon after lunch as I walked toward my office, Dick, the chief of the division, was coming down the hall in the opposite direction. He greeted me warmly and with some excitement in his voice said, "You are just the man I wanted to see. How would you like to go to Central America?"

I must have stammered and stuttered a bit because his next statement was, "I need you there immediately." Before I could utter any excuse about the new house, my wife and daughter in Pittsburgh, he said, "We have just had one of our case officers leave due to a serious illness in his family, and I want to replace him with you without any break of continuity."

Still stunned and wondering how I was going to broach this subject with Penny, I weakly said, "I will think about it, but I have to talk to my wife first."

Dick said, "Let me know first thing in the morning."

My telephone conversation with Penny that evening did not go well, particularly since she had her heart set on moving into our new house. This was particularly hard because we both loved the Washington area because of our friends there and also because of its proximity to her mother and other family. Nonetheless, Penny acquiesced and asked me to send her a State Department "post report" so that she could be thinking about how it was going to be to live there.

Fortunately, it took less than another week to finish the repairs, and we were able to rent the property to a couple about to be married. After taking a few more days for country and mission briefings, a physical, the appropriate inoculations and final paperwork for our assignment, I left Washington for Central America.

Central America

Only days after arriving in country, I became very busy and preoccupied with taking over the handling of the sources left by the departing case officer. I also had to find an appropriate apartment or condominium for my family. Every day ended with a long telephone conversation with Penny extolling how wonderful Central America was and that life there was much different and easier than our time in Mexico.

It was a dramatic change from the NOC assignment in Mexico with no overt association with the U.S. government. Penny and Amy joined me about a month later. We soon found a condominium in the central part of the city that we liked. Life was better and more secure than it had been in Mexico.

*****

My work tempo quickened after I developed and recruited two men close to the country's dictator. Neither of these sources could be seen associating with a U.S. person, therefore necessitating face-to-face meetings in nearby countries. I developed elaborate "cutout" mechanisms using coded telephone messages, secret writing hidden in innocuous letters and other techniques to ensure the safety of meetings with these men.

I traveled often and spent several days debriefing these sources, closed up in some hotel. Then I would return home for the report writing. Any information that was extremely urgent or perishable (meaning that time would overtake the information) was dispatched from the local CIA office.

Earthquakes in Central America were sometimes more danger-ous than the spy work. During one debriefing of a source the city where we were meeting was hit by a horrendous earthquake. The devastation was surreal and awful. Transportation and communica-tions were interrupted for everyone, and the government declared a state of emergency. Since our hotel was severely damaged, basically split into three parts and in danger of collapse, we tried to leave the city immediately, but were delayed due to the closure of the airport. My source, needing to get back home, used some high level contacts he had with the airport to get out on a military courier flight to his country. I followed a few days later as commercial flights began to return to service.

*****

The operating environment in country was extremely difficult because of the fishbowl-like size of the city, where everyone knew everyone, and the locals had a comprehensive intelligence network covering their own people as well as U.S. persons. Suffice it to say that these henchmen knew everything that moved and shook in the country.

The head of the local intelligence service also enjoyed the favor of the CIA and met regularly with us. I met with him on two occasions and must admit that his dark, blank eyes and unsmiling face struck terror to the marrow of my bones. I knew that this was a man who could kill me or anyone else and not blink an eye. Fortunately, my meetings with him were short and perfunctory, but on both occasions I went away feeling vulnerable and threatened. This was particularly so because he not only knew my identity along with my CIA affiliation, but he also knew where I lived with my family.

Almost a year later, one of my sources reported a particularly important piece of information. This information was tightly held, known only to the head of the government and two or three persons on the periphery, one of whom was my source.

Without notification to the station, a political decision at very high levels in Washington led to my source's information being released to Jack Anderson, a noted Washington newspaper reporter. The idea was to try to publicly embarrass the locals. The whole thing was ill-conceived. Anderson's by-line was also published in the Miami Herald, which was widely circulated in Central America.

A horrific Saturday morning meeting with my source began with him hitting me in the chest with the folded copy of the Miami Herald and yelling, "You have killed me! You have killed me!"

At that point I had no idea what he was talking about, but once I read the article I realized that he was completely compromised and had to leave the country immediately.

When I suggested that he leave the country with his family, he initially considered the idea, but for some unknown reason changed his mind and simply said, "I can't leave my country."

He withdrew into himself for a while, and we sat and looked at each other, knowing full well that if he remained there he would be killed. I was horrified at the prospect and kept encouraging him to leave. I argued that the CIA would take care of all of the arrangements and that we could effectively hide him and his family for an indefinite period of time. He steadfastly refused. We parted sadly.

Three days later, he was shot to death by unknown assailants.

The locals then turned their attention to me and another case officer who lived in the city proper and decided to have us arrested for conspiracy to undermine the government. Fortunately, some CIA sources were well placed in the government and we were tipped off early in the morning that the arrests were to take place.

Given about an hour to pack our important papers and a few things for the baby, Penny and I made our way to the airport to leave the country. We made our escape with just minutes to spare. Our two-year assignment came to a close, not as we had planned or thought it would, but once we safely arrived in Washington that evening, I received word that we were to be assigned next to Europe. I thought it was a fitting reward for a job well done and we were elated.

During my travels in Central Amercia, I had a chance meeting with Panamanian Roman Catholic Archbishop Marcos G. McGrath which developed into a long discussion about the church's position on birth control. After considerable debate and my dogged conviction that the women of the world, especially the poor ones, should make their own decisions about birth control, the archbishop half-jokingly suggested that perhaps I would make a better Anglican or Episcopalian than a Roman Catholic. About three weeks later, I happened to meet an Anglican priest when I was looking for a squash partner. Out of that new friendship and many long discussions about the two churches, came my decision to leave the Roman Catholic Church to become an Episcopalian. It was 1977.

Europe

I was met at the airport by my new boss, Jack. We made our way into the city and went directly to the historic district, where we had a wonderful lunch in an open air cafe. It was a bright, glorious sky with a warm sun to our backs. I had never met Jack, but I knew him by his reputation as a successful recruiter, linguist and a bon vivant.

He was born in Costa Rica. His father had worked for the United Fruit Company. Jack had inherited his father's large frame with strong arms and a big neck. But, he had his mother's refined looks and temperament. He was all Latin, to the core. Jack was gregarious and in love with life and his work. I especially liked those traits. Jack was also a respected case officer with the CIA's rank and file because he had been instrumental in the capture of Che Guevara in Bolivia.

We talked for several hours about the heavy presence of Cuban and Soviet intelligence activities in country. He cautioned me several times with examples of their extremely aggressive counter-intelligence activities and interests in U.S. citizens as well as station personnel. Jack explained that there were advantages to operating in one of Europe's largest cities because we could effectively use the subway system for counter-surveillance and "dusting off." He stressed it was imperative that I learn the subway system thoroughly and the locations of all the hotels that could be used for meeting sensitive sources.

Jack mentioned rather off-handedly, "The locals (meaning the intelligence service) already know who you are and they will know by tomorrow that you have arrived." We finished lunch and went to my hotel to drop my luggage.

I had not slept during the night flight from Washington and I was fading fast, wanting to go to bed. But Jack insisted that I stay up as long as I possibly could and retire at a normal hour. According to Jack, that would help me to get over jet lag quicker. He insisted that we visit the office. We arrived at about 5 p.m. and quickly passed through security to find our way to the elevators and up to the seventh floor.

A special code was required to get on the 7th floor and no other personnel were permitted there. Jack introduced me to the chief and deputy chiefs of the station, both of whom I had previously met, and the other officers, as we made our way to our section of the station. This was to be my new office, a small pair of rooms shared with Jack, an analyst, a secretary and one other case officer. "Nothing to write home about," I thought. We soon left the building, crossed the street and entered a bar. I noticed Jack was known to everyone in the bar. He was greeted as if he were Norm on *Cheers*, "*Jack!*" from everybody in the small corner bar.

*****

The work pace was different than that of Central America.

There was no sense of urgency or pressure to produce daily or hourly intelligence reports to the president of the United States or anyone else. Our major targets, the Soviets and Cubans, were well established and our work was more circumspect and driven by long-term development of well placed human assets (contacts).

The local people were enjoying their new-found freedom of expression and cultural experimentation. They were vibrant and exciting. They worked hard, but they also played hard and spent a great deal of time focused on their families and social responsibilities.

Penny and Amy arrived a couple of weeks later, and we immediately began sorting through the various flats I had looked at so that we could make our choice and get our furniture moved in.

The city is essentially apartments and condominiums, and Penny had some difficulty with our possible selections until we hit upon a beautiful third-floor flat in the north part of the city, not far from the office. The building was owned by a father and daughter. She was an architect and they were in the business of buying older buildings and refurbishing them. This three-story, six-flat building was one of their many properties. The floors in the flat were a beautiful hardwood with matching wood on all the window frames. There was a fireplace, a master bedroom and two smaller bedrooms, and two exquisite marble bathrooms. The hitch was that this apartment was not on our approved listing for housing and it was very expensive, "way above my pay grade."

I pled our case to the housing officer, who was not very sympathetic, for two reasons. First, he did not like CIA officers. He thought we were too aggressive and arrogant, and second, it cost too much for my rank. I offered to pay the difference out of pocket, but he remained adamant that we should continue to look for other less expensive places. Our prospective landlords were more than interested in having us lease from them because they wanted to get on the approved housing list to rent their other properties.

My task was to get a reduced price.

Several days later, Penny, Amy and I met with the daughter and her mother to look at the flat again. As I explained the situation to the daughter, her mother's attention turned to our daughter, Amy, who was then an adorable almost three-year-old with big blue eyes and strawberry blonde hair. It was love at first sight. The old woman was charmed and told her daughter, "This adorable child must live here, so do what you must."

The price came down, the office agreed and we were overjoyed. Our household goods were waiting in port, and we were soon moved in.

Within hours of moving in, we met our across-the-hall neighbors, John Lewis, the son of an Air Force general, and his British wife. They had four lovely daughters, two of whom were on either side of Amy. The couple was warm and welcoming and we became fast friends. We soon were socializing with their extended family as well as enjoying their company when we were at home. The property had a pool, and John Lewis and I often spent Saturday afternoons babysitting our children at the poolside.

*****

A significant part of our work was to meet "on-island" (Cubans living in Cuba) assets traveling from Cuba to Europe on either commercial or government business. Two of these sensitive assets, who were recruited years earlier by someone else, were turned over to me for handling. In both instances these men were allowed by the Cuban government to travel, but they often came with large delegations that always included security personnel to monitor them. These circumstances presented real challenges for face-to-face meetings and required detailed and exacting coordination and planning.

Communications with on-island sources were accomplished by mail. For example, the source would send a postcard to his "Aunt Jane" at an address of a person we had recruited to receive mail for us. Secret writing or codes in the text of the correspondence would signal his next visit to Europe.

After arriving, the source would go to a predesignated restaurant or café at a particular hour. I would be waiting. When visual contact was made and no surveillance detected, we would merge into the crowded subway system. Once near and in passing, I would hand him a note designating the meeting site. If for any reason he was unable to make the meeting, we would repeat the process the next day. This required checking in and out of hotels and remaining as inconspicuous as I could.

Security on these Cuban officials was stifling and it was difficult for them to get away from their security details for even short periods of time. In one particular case, the source was a Cuban government official who had traveled for many years to Europe. His security detail was often lax because they thought they knew him well and they would allow him to be alone "to go shopping." They, too, enjoyed the freedom to do their own shopping and visiting, so mid-afternoons were the best times for meetings. However, things do not always go the way one expects or plans.

This Cuban official, an on-island source, notified me that he would arrive in Europe with a trade delegation and would be available over three days for a meeting. He was to leave a chalk mark on a lamppost near a predesignated subway entrance. Two days passed without the chalk mark.

On the third day, the chalk mark was in its place, and I proceeded to the usual bar. When I entered the bar there was a large crowd, and my source was engaged in conversation with three or four people. We made eye contact, and he signaled that he was ready.

He made his excuses and left the bar. I left the bar, crossed the street and waited for him to descend into the opposite subway entrance. The objective here was for us to pass each other without stopping and for our hands to brush in a pass of the note.

As we proceeded toward each other on the subway platform, I noticed two security goons, one on his right and the second directly behind him. The source did not flinch, gave no signal to break off and continued to walk quickly toward me, seemingly without a concern.

I, on the other hand, was completely panicked but continued to move toward him. I saw his left hand drop to his side and his palm turn open and, almost instinctively, I passed the matchbook to him and collided into the security man following directly behind him. I said nothing and pushed on through the crowd. I was certain we had been discovered.

*****

The next two hours were among the most anxious in my professional life as I waited at the hotel. Right on time, the source arrived and once inside the door he said, "Man, that was close."

I asked why he had been surveilled so closely and had not been able to get rid of those goons. He said they were a new team and were not leaving him alone as others did on other trips. This raised real concerns for me. I was not convinced we had gotten away with that brush-pass. It was too close. I thought I might now have a double-agent operation on my hands. Nonetheless, I kept these concerns to myself for the time being.

We ordered lunch from room service and began our debriefing. A few years older than I, this contact was urbane, intelligent and not without ambition in his government. He also was married and had young children, one of whom needed a complicated surgery. His daughter's condition was part of his motivation for cooperating with the CIA. He had hoped we would somehow be able to arrange for her to have surgery in Europe. He did not trust the doctors and facilities in Cuba to handle her dire condition.

A great deal of our time was being eaten up with this discussion, and I wanted to move on to other matters, but I sensed that he was distraught by her deteriorating health, and he continued to push me for an answer. I was finally able to persuade him that something like this would require a great deal of preparation, and I would need a detailed plan from him outlining his cover and excuses to the Cuban government.

It would be no small matter to get his daughter out of Cuba for the surgery. I knew full well that the Castro regime had exceptional doctors. This kind of request would be out of order and would come under serious scrutiny by intelligence officials. Fortunately, the source was to return to Europe in a month, giving us both time to sort out the details of his request.

One of the most interesting things about recruiting people to do illegal or treasonous things was that those who agreed to cooperate often did so for mixed reasons. During my eight years of recruiting people to betray their countries, one motive seemed more common than others. An official, a relative or friend who felt unappreciated or demeaned by someone like Castro or other official was more likely to cooperate with us.

Recruiting was not so much about bagging a big target like Raul Castro but, rather, looking at those closest to them and then moving out from the inner circle to other friends and relatives who could be more easily contacted. Often, I would sit at my desk drawing a bull's eye with the target in the center, then listing associates, friends and family on concentric circles to be studied for vulnerabilities or access.

The simplest way to get access or a snapshot of a target, more often than not, was to meet government officials or businessmen who dealt with Cubans or Soviets. On occasion, I would be fortunate enough to innocently meet someone in a social setting who had traveled to Cuba. Often, these persons were easily persuaded to collect general information about the economy, levels of security and the observable health of people like the Castro brothers or any other Cubans they came in contact with.

*****

The first year of our assignment to Europe was a settling-in time and we thoroughly enjoyed our new surroundings and the culture. We had a lovely home, lots of friends and diversions and some travel on long weekends to other parts of Europe.

I attended every bullfight I could, often taking my boss, Jack, and in turn, our daughters on occasion. Amy, now four years old, accompanied me to many off-season bullfights. The crowds were small and the tickets cheap, so we were often in the front rows of the ring, becoming somewhat of an object of curiosity for the Spaniards who regularly attended those *corridas*.

During one fight, as the bullfighter circled the ring, celebrating his triumph, and folks threw hats, cigars and roses to him as he made his merited *vuelta* of the plaza, Amy spontaneously threw her Teddy bear to him. The matador picked up the Teddy bear, kissed it, saluted Amy, walked to the fence and returned the bear to her. The small crowd went crazy with cheers and applause, not exactly the attention a clandestine CIA operative wanted.

As good as life was in Europe, Penny had begun to grow restless and unhappy with my travel to other places to meet sources and support clandestine operations elsewhere. She felt increasingly isolated because of difficulties with the language.

Our circle of friends, while supportive and fun to be with, could also be tiresome and boorish. Most often, the parties we attended or had at our home were for purposes of assessing, developing and recruiting persons to do spy work. Penny once pleaded, "Could we have or go to just one party where you are not trying to recruit somebody? I wish we had <u>real</u> friends."

Adding to the problem was that she was now pregnant with our second child and was deeply concerned about the prospect of having the baby in Europe without her mother present. Penny longed to go home to the States.

I, on the other hand, was having a wonderful time. As the months passed, however, I could tell that there was no consoling

Penny or deflecting her desire to return to the States. I, too, had now become disenchanted, not with Europe, but by what was happening inside the CIA.

President Jimmy Carter had appointed his Naval Academy classmate and friend, Admiral Stansfield Turner, to be director of the CIA. A worse choice could not have been made, at least for those of us in the clandestine service or Deputy Directorate for Operations (DDO). Admiral Turner had little or no regard or understanding of the value of human intelligence collection. He believed that technical coverage, meaning electronic and satellite surveillance, was all that was needed to know our enemies. He believed that the diplomats could deal with the hearts and minds of foreign government leaders.

Admiral Turner began to dismantle the DDO and retire or reassign a great many of us. Morale could not have been lower, and many of the best of the cold warriors were heading for the door. Many of us who were in the trenches and putting ourselves at risk for our country had little faith in President Carter's or Turner's leadership. There were a number of intelligence failures and operational disasters. I also harbored a great deal of bitterness about what had happened to my source in Central America.

When the news came late into the second year of our tour in Europe that the FBI was interested in hiring me, these other factors weighed heavily in my decision to say yes and move on.

10 ╬

Discovery

Penny and I drove from Memphis to Nashville, Tennessee, on a bright, beautiful April morning, not knowing what the outcome of this trip would be. We had come to what seemed a dead end in our legal efforts to force the state of Tennessee to open my adoption record. Our attorney, Jim, had worked for six months to find a way to legally challenge the sealing of the records, but without any luck. He was completely frustrated with the Tennessee Bureau of Vital Statistics, which had, he said, "put us into a Catch-22 situation."

Jim explained that we had to sue the state to open the records. Tennessee law stipulated that a suit for the opening of adoption records had to be filed with the court that originally ordered the adoption. He said the attorneys for Vital Statistics took the position that the whole of the adoption record was sealed, to include the court of record, and therefore they would not tell us where and when the adoption had taken place.

Jim said he did get a hint from one of the attorneys that Tennessee might not even have the records, so he had contacted the Kentucky Bureau of Vital Records, since my father was from Kentucky. Kentucky took an even harder line on adoption records, refusing to be sued in such cases.

Jim said that he was sorry he had failed. He was giving up our cause. "No charges to you since I do not believe anyone should pay for failure." He assured me that he thought I was entitled under the law to sue, but without knowing the court of record, no suit could be filed, which was "clearly an unfair, Catch-22 situation," he complained. Then he said a funny thing: "I know you are some kind of spy or interrogator for the government, so I suggest you go to the Bureau of Vital Statistics in Nashville, mustering all of your spy skills and try to persuade someone, anyone, to give us any information that would help resolve this impasse. Otherwise, this is a dead issue."

We arrived in Nashville precisely at 9 a.m., found the Bureau of Vital Statistics easily and parked the car. As we entered the main building, I noticed signage for birth certificates and we went into that office. Once I told the clerk that I was looking for an adoption record, she immediately summoned a file supervisor. A knowing glance towards Penny, "now the hassle begins." It made my stomach tighten.

A lovely, soft-spoken woman in her mid-fifties soon appeared, introduced herself and asked how she might help us. In an almost pleading fashion, I told her about my lawyer's failed efforts and that we wanted the records opened for medical history since we had had a serious health problem with our daughter Amy.

She moved us off to a more private area in the office because I became emotional and began to tear up. Much to my surprise, this woman appeared sympathetic. She listened attentively, taking an occasional note; she asked questions gently and nodded affirmatively when I expressed frustration with the situation we were in.

She told us she would verify whether an adoption had indeed occurred and what information the Vital Statistics held with respect to an adoption decree. Asking us to wait for a few minutes so that she could find my record, she left and we waited.

When she returned, she asked us to step out into the corridor so we could have more privacy. She said she had confirmed my story, and she herself could not understand why I could not be told, at the very minimum, about the court of record. She told us she was willing to speak to the legal staff to try to persuade them to release that specific information. I asked if she might allow me to speak with the attorneys personally, but she demurred, saying that it would be best if she did that herself.

This amazing woman disappeared down the corridor and we waited there shuffling our feet and fretting about her chances for success for what seemed an eternity.

She returned in 20 or 30 minutes and whispered, "The lawyers have agreed that you are in an impossible position and they have relented. I am authorized to tell you that you were adopted on February 16, 1946, in Danville, Kentucky. Circuit Judge Gilbert White issued the adoption order."

We were dumbfounded.

In her hands she held a thick volume of birth certificates with a large white tab marking a place. She asked us to move to the side of the corridor and gently said, "I am going to open the book to your birth certificate. Listed on the back in pencil are the names of every person or institution that has ever asked for a copy of your birth certificate."

She said, "The name of the first person who received your certificate is shown at the top of the page. It is customary in adoption cases that the lawyer representing the adopting parents was the first person to receive a newly issued birth certificate."

She noted that the first issuance of my birth certificate in the name John Perry Smith was sent out approximately two weeks after the adoption decree. She said that we should pay particular attention to that first name, and then, scan quickly the rest of the names to see if we recognized any of them. She turned the page and my eyes went directly to the first notation. It read Joe Davis, Esq., Danville, Kentucky.

There were approximately 16 other notations on the back of the certificate, all of which I recognized as schools or U.S. Government agencies, which had required certified copies. She went on to say that the only absolutely true data about me on the new birth certificate were the date and place of birth. She assured us that I was born in Knoxville, Tennessee, on October 21, 1944.

However, the most remarkable fact revealed by this gracious and generous woman was to confirm the court of record, which, indeed, was where my adopting parents had been living, and where I had spent the first four years of my life.

We were greatly moved by this kind woman's sympathetic and generous assistance. I wondered if she had really consulted the bureau's lawyers. Or had she alone made the decision to give us this important information? However she made her decision to help us, it was full of grace. I was effusive in my thanks as we said goodbye. Her eyes moistened as she hugged us and wished us luck.

Penny and I ran from the building, realizing that we had to drive directly to Danville, Kentucky, which would take about four and a half to five hours. It was Friday and about 11:30 a.m., and we were certain the courthouse in Danville would close at 4:30 or 5 p.m.

We raced to Danville, filled with great joy and a hope-filled expectation of discovery. We arrived at the county courthouse at about 4:30 p.m.

When we entered the Clerk of the Court's office, there was an elderly man seated at the front counter. He seemed bored and then irritated that we had come so near to closing time, telling us that he closed promptly at 5 p.m. I told him we wanted to see the court records from February 16, 1946, in the cases decided by Judge Gilbert White.

He responded in an almost curt way that the ledgers containing those court filings were at the rear of the room. He said we needed only to look for the date stamped on the cover to find the correct volume. He made no offer to help. We walked quickly to the rear of the room and began our search, finding the volume we wanted right away.

As I opened the book to February 1946, and began looking for February 16, we were shocked that there was no corresponding page or entry. Could there be a mistake? Had we misunderstood what we were told? I panicked and uttered some obscenity. The old man got up from his chair and joined us at the rack of ledgers. He solemnly asked if there was a problem.

I said anxiously that we were looking for the court record of February 16, but there was none in the book. He took a quick look at the dates on the two pages we were fixed on, and he said, "There is no record because February 16, 1946, was a Saturday, and Judge White did not hold court on Saturdays, except for adoption cases.

"Are you people looking for an adoption record?" he asked in a condescending tone, which read "are you completely stupid?"

"We are," I said.

He replied, without any hint of regret or sympathy, "Adoption records have been removed from all of the county seats in Kentucky and locked up under seal in Frankfort, to keep people like you from discovering your biological parents."

I was horrified by his comment and began to argue that I had a right to see those records, that I should be entitled to sue, that I needed those records for medical purposes. He closed the book and said, "Frankfort will never open those records. I'm sorry."

Devastated, I looked at Penny, and she took my arm and moved me toward the way we had come in. The old man began walking with us to return to his seat. He sat down, and we took a few more steps toward the door.

As an afterthought, I asked him, "Is there a lawyer, Joe Davis, in this town?"

The clerk said, "The best damn lawyer in town, Sonny; he is right across the street."

I impatiently replied, "I'm not looking for Joe Davis, Jr., or Joe Davis, III. We need the Joe Davis who was here in 1946."

The old man answered, "As I said, Sonny, the best damn lawyer in town, Joe Davis, is across the street."

Then, surprisingly, he asked if he could call him for us. It took only a few seconds for the old man to tell Joe Davis he was sending us over to talk with him.

Mr. Davis met us at the door of his office. He was a pleasant man, tall and slender, with an air of calm and certainty-- a Southern gentleman through and through. Although in his later years, perhaps near eighty, his mind was keen and he moved with ease.

I explained why we were there. Mr. Davis said that the records from his early years had been retired to the basement of his home. However, he said, he had an index of every case he had handled over his many years of practicing law in Danville. He produced a black, three-ringed, loose-leaf notebook. This held his index. Every case was noted by its legal name on the left with a date of completion. On the right was some sort of code, which turned out to be the box number where the file was stored.

Mr. Davis said he would go home, retrieve the record and bring it back to his office. He left. We waited in silence almost as if we were afraid to break the spell of what was unfolding before us. Was this incredible luck? Amazing grace, if there ever was…a God thing. "Please, God, let him find the file."

As promised, about 15 minutes later, Mr. Davis returned to his office and placed a folder on a table in front of us. As he placed it on the table, he said, "Son, I hope this will help you."

We stared at the folder, closed on the table. I could not wait to open it, but I was afraid. Mr. Davis started to walk from the room, and just as he neared the door, he turned and said, "You may have anything in the folder that you wish; however, please make copies of everything you take and leave them with me." Then he disappeared into the next room.

The first document in the folder was a legal decree setting forth the circumstances of my adoption. Also in the folder was my original birth certificate--my first birth certificate. It was shocking to see that I was first known as William Clarence Woolum. My mother was still married to Reuben Woolum at the time of my birth in 1944, hence I was surnamed Woolum. However, the 1946 decree narrative was the most helpful because it detailed my biological mother's circumstances at that time.

According to the adoption decree, my mother was 33 years old when I was born. She had three other children, all girls, but had since divorced their father, Reuben Woolum. We also noted that she had lived on Highland Avenue in Danville, Kentucky, which was the same street on which my adopting parents had lived. She was also born in Danville. My adopting father was born in Somerset, Kentucky, just a few short miles south of Danville. The decree also stated that my father was unknown. My mother's maiden name was Preston.

We decided to take the entire file and leave Mr. Davis with copies of all the documents. We bid farewell to Mr. Davis with many thanks and left his office. We paused outside his office, absolutely emotionally spent, but determined to press on.

The plan now was to find a motel, eat something and begin to search for my mother, Wynetta Preston. Finally checked in at a motel, and having eaten for the first time since breakfast, we looked through the Danville phone book and discovered there were 54 listings of Prestons. I began to call.

Every Preston listened to my short story, which began, "My

name is John Perry Smith and I am looking for Wynetta Preston, my mother. Do you know her whereabouts?" I heard suspicion in the voices and all of my inquiries were rebuffed, but more often than not these folks referred me to Jimmy Preston, the owner of Preston Funeral Home in downtown Danville.

Several phone calls to Jimmy Preston's residence determined that he was at the country club for a late dinner. Almost frantic, I kept making calls and pleading for help. Finally, at about 10:45 p.m., Jimmy Preston returned my messages and we talked. I told him who I was and that I was looking for Wynetta Preston.

He responded, "Yes, I know your mother. She was here very recently. And by the way, you have great looking sisters."

Preston was cheerful and almost elated to be involved in such a discovery. I asked him for Wynetta's phone number. He told me that my mother lived three hours south of Danville in Tennessee, but that she had a half brother, Joe Coomer, in Danville. He preferred that I contact the half brother and get her contact information from him. Preston promised that if the half brother would not or could not provide that information then he would make an effort to broker an introduction.

It was getting late and I wanted to push on. I called the number Preston provided and the woman answering the phone gasped when I told her my name and she immediately asked where I was calling from.

"You know me?" I asked.

"Of course I know you. You are John, Wynetta's son," she cheerfully answered.

When I asked how she knew me, she responded, "I have known you since the day you were born," but no real explanation followed. She excitedly told me her name was Edna and that she was married to Joe Coomer, but all of that was unimportant at that moment.

"You must call your mother right now," she urged. Edna repeated Mother's telephone number twice and insisted I call her as soon as I hung up the phone.

"Your mother will be so happy. She wants to know you, John. She has wanted to know you her whole life."

I promised I would call. We said goodbye.

I sat down on the edge of the bed and took a long, deep breath. Penny and I talked for about 15 minutes, debating the pros and cons of continuing.

Not one thing in the day had persuaded us to do anything else but to move forward and meet my mother.

At 11 p.m., I telephoned Wynetta Preston in Wartburg, Tennessee. A soft, quiet voice answered the phone.

I said, "My name is John Perry Smith and I have reason to believe that you know me."

She replied, "Yes. You were born on October 21st, 1944, at 4:15 in the morning."

I could hardly breathe. I didn't know whether to cry, scream and shout, or merely fade into silence.

She asked where I was, and I said, "In your hometown of Danville."

She said, "I will be up there in the morning."

"No. We have a lot to talk about before we meet," I replied anxiously. Her calm was disarming.

"You must meet your sisters," her voice rising on a cheerful note.

"My sisters? They know about me?"

"Of course they know about you. I have never kept you a secret. Please let me come up there tomorrow. We will talk then."

Again, I said that there was too much for us to discuss before we made a decision to see one another. She refused to accept that notion and insisted that we meet.

"I have waited so long to see you again." Her voice was even, but I heard her sincerity and joy. She was glad that I had contacted her.

We talked for some 20 to 30 minutes, and what struck me during this short conversation was that she spoke to me as if I had never been out of her presence. She was calm and confident that I had made the right decision to look for her. I was reassured about meeting her.

We agreed Penny and I would come to her home the following morning between 10:30 and 11 a.m. She said it would take approximately three hours to drive the distance.

Again, she insisted my sisters and "the rest of the family" would want to meet me. I again resisted that idea. So I suggested that rather than meeting with a large group of people, she and I should have some private time first.

She finally relented and said to come as planned and we would have some free time before meeting the rest of the family. We said our goodbyes and she admonished me to drive carefully.

"How odd," I thought, "coming from someone who did not know me--she had to be my mother."

There were a thousand unanswered questions and the next day was filled with promise. Finally, I would have the answers I so wanted. Penny and I went to bed and tried to sleep. We were restless and slept very little, talking over what we thought we would learn during the coming day. I tried to imagine what my mother looked like. Why did she insist that I meet my sisters almost immediately?

At about 4:30 a.m., I told Penny we had to get going to Wartburg. She persuaded me to write out some of the questions to which I wanted specific answers. This helped to stall me a bit, and she prevailed about having breakfast. I had to admit, it would have seemed a little odd to show up on my mother's doorstep at 7 a.m.

It was an easy but mountainous drive down State Route 27 from Danville to Wartburg, Tennessee. In truth, it is about a three-hour drive of considerable beauty through the Cumberland Plateau and Highlands. However, on this day, it was a fast blur. We arrived in about two hours and ten minutes. I wanted only to see my mother.

Her small, white wooden-framed house was on Main Street. The lawn was well manicured. Looking for some reassurance from Penny as we approached the house, I turned to her and she nodded for me to go forward. There was now only a screen door separating me from my mother.

We knocked, and a young girl, in her teens, came to the door.

She warmly greeted us and said, "Granny has gone to get her hair done. She should be home soon. Please come in and wait. I am your niece, Sandy." There it was again--calmness and an easy, natural familiarity.

"Granny has gone to have her hair done because she wanted to look her best when you arrived. She should be home shortly," she said.

"Niece? I have a niece?" I silently pondered. She offered sodas or lemonade, telling us to make ourselves comfortable.

My eyes scanned the room, looking for photographs or anything that would give me clues as to where I had come from. Then I noticed an elderly woman sitting on a sofa at the end of the room, clad in a summer print dress, with her hands neatly folded in her lap. She smiled pleasantly at us but said nothing.

"She is your Granny White, your grandmother," my niece said with a reverent tone. "She doesn't say much."

I said, "Hello," and extended my hand. She took my hand, held it tenderly, smiled and said, "I know you."

The investigator I had become would not allow me to stop asking questions. Sandy was patient but realized I was anxious and she said repeatedly, "Granny will be here soon. She will tell you the story." This young girl, my new-found blood relative, showed that same composure and quiet assurance that I had heard in my mother's voice the night before, and it was confounding. I wondered: Is it a family trait?

After about an hour's wait, my mother appeared in the doorway, smiling broadly, with joyful eyes. A long, warm hug followed.

I was stunned to see someone I looked like. I could not get over how our physical characteristics were so similar. I kept looking at her eyes, the way she spoke, the tone of her voice, her mannerisms and all that made this tiny little woman my mother.

There was no need for any uncertainty or reservation. No DNA test was necessary. There was no mistake. This was, indeed, my mother. We settled down in the dining room for sandwiches, drinks and a long conversation.

My new family. My wife Penny at my right shoulder and my mother, Wynetta, on my left. Left to right: Bobbie, Betty and JoAnn, my three half-sisters.

11 ⌗

Wynetta's Story

Mother began almost reverently, "Your father was Clarence Bullen. He died in the late 1960s of a stroke. I have several pictures of him to show you."

As Penny and I looked at the photographs, Mother identified others who were with him, and she tried to give us the approximate dates of the pictures. Two of the photographs were of particular interest. The first because it was a Bullen family portrait: mom, dad and the children, five in all. The second one showed my father seated on a sofa entertaining one of his grandnieces about a year before he died.

"Your father was living with his younger brother Hugh and his wife, Cora Mae, when he died. They took care of him after his first stroke four years before his death. He was alone except for them."

The sounds of Bullen and Woolum ricocheted through my head. Who was who? I asked Mother for more background. She said that in the mid-1930s in her hometown of Danville, she met and became fast friends with Edna Woolum. Edna was from Wartburg, Tennessee, and had married a railroad man from Danville. The irony was almost too much to bear; John Smith was the consummate railroader and from Danville as well. Edna's brother, Reuben Woolum, frequently came to Danville and Cincinnati, Ohio, to find work when he was not farming.

A courtship ensued almost immediately after Edna introduced Wynetta and Reuben. They married in 1937 and Reuben took his new bride back to Wartburg to the Woolum farm to start a family. One year later, JoAnn was born, quickly followed by Bobbie and Betty. Life on the farm in a narrow hollow in a smaller chain of the Great Smoky Mountains was hard. The Great Depression hit Appalachia with a vengeance.

"We were poor dirt farmers, barely making it," Mother said. "Reuben brought his mother into our home and she began to run the house. I had to cook breakfast every morning, tend to the girls, clean the house and raise a garden in the spring and summer. It was very difficult and I did not like all of the commotion and confusion--Reuben and his brothers drink'n, fuss'n and fight'n every time they got a little money."

Reuben had heard about work in Oak Ridge from a good many folks from Wartburg who had begun to make the twenty-six mile trip to make better money. Reuben, with an eighth-grade education, did not qualify for any job he might have wanted, but Wynetta did. Mother remembered:

"I went to work in 1943 in Oak Ridge at the Y-12 plant to make some extra money. Y-12 was making the first atomic bomb, even though we really didn't know at the time that's what we were doing. It was a very secret and guarded plant. Reuben wanted me to work there because there were good-paying jobs for people with a high-school diploma, which I had. I got a job as a cashier in the cafeteria because I was always good with numbers and I could make change quickly. I met your father, who was a bus driver who drove workers from Wartburg to Oak Ridge each day. He was kind to me and I needed some kindness at that time."

I interrupted to ask why my birth certificate said that Reuben Woolum was my father and gave me the name William Clarence Woolum.

"I was still married to Reuben," Mother answered. She added with some pride, "You were named William in memory of my grandfather. Your middle name Clarence was for your father. I loved your father."

Mother paused, sighed ever so softly and tried to clarify her long ago dilemma, "I thought your father loved me because he said he did, but when he found out I was pregnant, he left me. I also learned that he had lied about being divorced from his wife, Ruby. They had separated, but they were not divorced. So, it was hard, but it was good that he left," she said, her voice trailing off in the memory of it all.

As Mother told it, she was essentially run off because of Reuben's drinking and carousing, and his determination to "raise these girls like country girls, not citified children." She said Reuben thought country folk were the "salt of the earth."

"In other words," she mocked, "they were better than city folk." She alleged that he told her not to worry about raising the children.

"Me and Ma can raise the girls just fine without you," he said.

Mother told Reuben, "That's what you've been doing anyway,

so keep on doing it!" Her tone hardened with the words.

Mother recalled that Reuben was furious at the news of her affair with Clarence and forced her out of the house. She said she did not blame him nor did she want to continue living with him, his mother and the other sons on the farm. She moved to Oak Ridge and lived with her best girlfriend, who also worked at Y-12.

Life began to be better even though she was pregnant and Clarence had left. I mentally noted Mother was giving an alternative account of why she left Reuben and the girls.

"There was an FBI Agent who was responsible for security in our area of the plant. He watched everything that was going on and made sure the workers did not talk about their responsibilities when taking their meals. He was a proper, kind man and he often complimented me on my ability to count and make change, moving my line along a lot faster than the other girls working there. I sensed that he liked me, so when I began I began to 'show' with you I told him the whole story and asked what I should do."

Mother stressed that she told the FBI Agent she was going to have "this baby" no matter what. He was sympathetic and wanted to help, so he suggested she take a leave of absence, have the baby and then come back to work when she was able.

"He said he would speak to my supervisor, assuring me I would have my job back when I was ready, because I was a good, honest worker."

Accordingly, Wynetta Woolum took a leave of absence from Y-12. She was six months pregnant.

During the war years, the city of Oak Ridge was a "closed

town," heavily guarded and secured because of the bomb project. Mother could no longer live there during her leave, so she moved to Knoxville, taking a basement-level one-bedroom apartment. She worked cleaning people's homes and doing alterations for the wealthier women who came to an expensive dress shop where she worked part-time.

In a letter to me dated June 6, 1978, barely a month and a few days after our reunion, Mother wrote, "…I saved my money to pay your hospital and doctor bills. I didn't ask anyone for any help. My mother was in the hospital where she spent most of her life and my brother was in the service. My dad was dead. So really I didn't have anyone to go to."

She said that she also feared the stigma of my being an illegitimate child in a small town where no secrets are hidden.

Reading and rereading this letter over the years has always given me pause because she says, "I saved my money to pay your hospital and doctor bills." (Emphasis added).

Was she blameless in this pregnancy? Were they not her or our bills?

Mother also wrote in the same letter, "When I found out I was going to have you, I wasn't unhappy about it. All I could think about was that I would have a baby that no one could tell me what to do with it." This became her mantra.

Over the next thirty years I was to have with Mother, she must have repeated a thousand times, "While I was carrying you, I would say to myself that this is my baby, and no one is going to tell me what to do with it."

It was her way of rejecting Reuben's conviction that the children, their girls, should be raised as "country girls" rather than being "citified," as Mother was brought up. It also helped to justify giving me to the Smiths for adoption. Mother was fond of saying, "I wanted to give you better than I had." I recognized yet another shift or paradox in her reasoning, but I left it unchallenged.

Mother was surprised to learn that I did not know I was adopted until my tenth year.

After hearing about the Halloween incident, she said, "That's why Yuma stopped writing and sending me photographs of you."

Then she showed us my school pictures from grades one through six. I was shocked to see those familiar pictures, copies of which I have in a family album. She insisted that she was reluctant to give me up for adoption, and even after she had agreed with the Smiths and the court to do so, she claimed that she would have wanted to take me back if the Smiths could not have managed. She reasoned:

"Now I understand. She was afraid you would look for us. I told Yuma and John at the time of the adoption that if they were not able to take care of you they should bring you back to me. I never heard from Yuma again, but Yuma was in touch with Edna, Reuben's sister, so I knew you had gone to California. I also knew she died. I wondered about you…what you would do now that you were alone."

My two mothers knew each other from Danville and their mutual friend, Edna, who became the broker for my adoption. Mother resumed work a few weeks after I was born, finding a baby sitter for me during the day. Mother said that when she picked me up in the evening she realized I was being neglected, because I had frequent diaper rash, was always hungry and very clingy.

She wrote in June 1978, "With all of this I can't remember feeling sorry for myself. My thoughts and plans were for you. After you were borned (sic), you was such a loving baby and you didn't cry much. But I knew you needed love. I would put you in the bed with me and you would pat my face until you went to sleep. This was the reason it was so hard for me to give you up. But your welfare was more important than my feelings."

Mother and Edna visited each other often, and seeing the situation for what it was, Edna began to encourage Mother to give me up for adoption, specifically to the Smiths since John and Yuma Smith were well known to them as good people.

"I met with Yuma many times and she was desperate to have you. She and John had been married a long time and were not able to have a child. They both had good jobs and were educated. I knew they would be able to give you a better life."

My mind drifted into thinking that things were beginning to make sense, but I had a thousand questions. Why hadn't Yuma Smith told me this story? It was not so awful… so shameful. Then Mother jarred me back to the moment as she began to characterize Yuma and John Smith:

"Getting you was what Yuma wanted and she did all the talking. I am not sure about John because he never said a word during the three or four times we all got together to talk about you, except for the day I gave you to them. They came to the house to get you, and as I handed you to Yuma, I started to cry."

"John touched my shoulder and said, 'Wynetta, you have done real good up to now. Don't worry; we will give him a good home.' I turned away and they left quickly. You were about six months old. I didn't see you again until the court in Danville had the final hearing in 1946. After that, Yuma kept me up with you with occasional letters and your school photographs."

Her comments prompted a direct, hard question from me, "Are you sure that John Smith was not my biological father?" My adopting mother's deathbed remarks about John Smith's long-term infidelity haunted me and I wanted the truth.

"Clarence Bullen was your birth father, not John Smith. That is the absolute truth," she firmly replied. I relaxed.

*****

Several hours had passed and a crowd had begun to gather in the far end of the house. Lots of chatter began to waft into our hearing. Mother said it was my sisters, actually half sisters, and their children, eager to meet us. So we stopped our conversation to meet my sisters and their families.

It all quickly became a blur with names: Bobbie, her current husband John, and two daughters by two other marriages; Betty with her current man, Sammy, and her two children by two different men; and finally, JoAnn, married only once with two children. For someone who had few remaining relatives from the Smith clan, the immediate result of our discovery was that I now had fifty-some new kin in Morgan County, Tennessee.

They wanted to hear everything…my life story…why I had not "come home" before.

Home? My home was with Penny and Amy and we lived in Europe.

There was an immediate familiarity and intimacy that was electric, but also surreal and baffling. Most surprising to me was that Mother had never made a secret of me and that my sisters knew my name and generally what had happened to me up until California.

JoAnn said, "I always knew you were out there and I wanted to know you, my whole life. It would make me cry that we couldn't know you."

I was stunned by their sincerity and warmth. I was the prodigal son, come home.

The afternoon rolled into evening with no break in questions and conversation. Out of nowhere the dining room table and folding card tables were set, food put on them and beverages served. There were people in every corner of the house eating, talking, questioning and rejoicing.

It was an amazing day, beginning with fear and trepidation, and then, being welcomed with open arms and hearts by people I had never known, but who had known about me. It was astounding to both Penny and me that they treated me as if I were always theirs, but somehow away…on a long journey or in military service.

After considerable discussion about where Penny and I would stay the night, we opted for the small motel next door to Mother's house. It was a good idea because we were exhausted and needed some time to ourselves, to regroup and think about the incredible events of our discovery. We fell into the bed, so tired and excited we were unable to sleep much.

*****

Day two began with breakfast with Mother and my sisters. In my concern for clarity and facts, I asked if we could construct a family tree. Mother agreed, but had some news she wanted to share. She said that earlier in the morning she had spoken to my father's brother, Raymond, and he and his family wanted to meet us later that afternoon. Penny and I were flabbergasted Mother had acted so quickly and without asking us, but we were also curious to meet the younger brother of my father. All present assured us "they were good people and everything would be fine" with our meeting. So the meeting was on.

Mother started her narrative after the breakfast dishes were done. I took notes and we were careful to get the genealogy down as best we could. Surprisingly, she also knew a great deal about my father's family since they had been long-time residents of Wartburg and she was able to complete some of my paternal roots.

As Mother narrated her life and the family tree began to take shape, she recalled events as they related to people she identified; some were good and some were pretty ugly.

Wynetta Preston was born in 1913 at Danville, Kentucky, but in her infancy the family moved to Cincinnati, Ohio. Her mother, Annie, and father, Robert, apparently had a good marriage and they were happy until Robert's death. Annie subsequently married Joe Coomer and had a son, Joe.

Mother's grandmother lived about a block away and Mother said that her grandmother essentially raised her from about age one to twelve, since they spent many afternoons and evenings together. Mother said she never felt safe at home with Coomer and preferred staying with her grandmother. "Pretty much living there," she stressed.

One spring afternoon after school Mother was getting ready to go to her grandmother's house. Coomer, who she thought was asleep in another room, broke the latched door to her bedroom and attempted to rape her, only to be prevented by a neighbor who heard her screams for help and interrupted the assault. The neighbor took Mother to her grandmother's home so that she would be safe.

When Wynetta's mother returned home from work that evening and learned what had happened, she confronted Coomer and he unashamedly admitted he had assaulted Wynetta. Yet, he refused to leave their home. A quarrel ensued and Wynetta's grandmother took control of the situation and insisted that Wynetta come to live with her permanently. Wynetta was able to visit her mother often when Coomer was at work or away.

A year later Wynetta's grandmother died. "It was the worst day of my life because I had to go back to my mother and I was no longer safe," she remembered. For three years she said she endured crude, drunken attempts to molest her. The marriage finally ended in divorce.

Annie was not a woman to remain single for long and she soon married John White, uncle to Reuben Woolum. John White was a hard-drinking wife beater who made their life a living hell. White often beat Wynetta's mother and was menacing and threatening most of the time. Wynetta lived in constant fear and vigilance, wanting only to escape, since her mother could not or would not get rid of their tormentor.

Some years later White, in a drunken rage, threw Wynetta's mother "across the room into a wall, where she landed like a rag doll, doing some damage to her brain." Wynetta said, "Mother had to be institutionalized and was never the same."

Wynetta married when she was sixteen to escape the horrors of her life. She married Bill, a forty-year-old traveling salesman.

"Other than my father, he was the first man who was nice to me," she said. After a few months, the road trips and motels grew tiresome and difficult, so they agreed to divorce and Wynetta moved back to Cincinnati, where she found work in a ladies dress shop. There she learned sewing and became an accomplished seamstress and dressmaker.

Mother's story was heartbreaking and painful for us to hear, but she was able somehow to tell her story calmly and without much emotion. There was an occasional change in her tone, more intense and just slightly angry, when she spoke of Reuben's abuses, but as for the rest of the narration, she was neutral.

There was, however, something that she said several times that was a clue to one of her defense mechanisms: "When I found that I was not loved or wanted, I would just leave and never look back. There was no need to fuss or fight about it. I would just go on with my life."

It was lunchtime and, again magically, tables were set and food came from somewhere. Canned green beans, tomatoes, corn, assorted greens and freshly baked corn bread filled the table. Sweet iced tea was everybody's preferred drink. Water or coffee were the only other options. My mother, sisters, two brothers-in-law, Penny and I sat down at a large table, and grandchildren came and went in the background, grabbing food and chatting among themselves.

I noticed Grandma White sat on the sofa at a TV tray with a plate of food someone had prepared for her and ate by herself. I asked why she did not join us at the table and Mother said coldly,

"She is fine there." I noted her tone and wondered why. One of the grandchildren sat close to her and lovingly attended to her. I learned later that the granddaughter was Leah, a child who for her own reasons had become Granny White's caretaker, when she came out of the "mental home" for visitations.

Annie White, with the most pleasant countenance I think I had ever seen, had sat on that sofa for two days... listening or not... and had said nothing in my hearing except for when I greeted her and she said simply, "I know you."

Lunch ended with the same efficiency as the setting of the table. Everything was cleaned up, put away, and before we knew it we were in the car and off to meet Raymond and Ruth Bullen.

12 ⧉

The Bullen Clan

Raymond and Ruth Bullen received us warmly into their modest home at the edge of Wartburg. Raymond was a retired railroad man, farmer and land speculator. He had made substantial money buying remote land and strip-mining it. He had an open and kind face weathered by years of outdoor work and hard labor. His frame was slight and his manner was relaxed and gentle. I searched his eyes for some spark of mirth or semblance of our common heritage or lineage. He was my father's youngest brother and perhaps closest to my father when he was alive. I asked what I should call him, and he replied, "Raymond or Uncle Raymond, since I am your uncle."

"No denial here," I thought.

Ruth Redmon Bullen was a handsome woman with dark eyes and dark hair, but her face showed the strain of raising children, working a farm and attending to her husband. She was shy and more retiring than Raymond, but she was genuine and sweet as she served iced tea and freshly baked apple pie. "Made from scratch, just like my mother's," she said with some pride. It was delicious.

It became quickly obvious that my sister, JoAnn, was close to the Bullen family. I could see the respect and affection between her and Ruth. JoAnn told the story of how Ruth's father had given JoAnn her first job in his small grocery store when she was 12 years old. JoAnn and Ruth had known each other all their lives, and Raymond and Ruth's children, Colin, Charles and Alice, had been schoolmates and friends. I wondered what it was like to have lived in one place your whole life and to still see your childhood friends.

Surprisingly, Ruth led the discussion about how Clarence, my father, had lived out his last years semi-comatose from a major stroke and how he was cared for by another brother, Hugh, and his wife, Cora Mae. My father apparently lingered almost four years before having the second stroke that killed him.

As Ruth told the story, I noted a sadness in her voice that revealed she felt sorry for Clarence as he essentially wasted away before their very eyes, dying with nothing and no one. It was, however, also clear that she was not sympathetic to the way he had treated the women in his life, particularly his wife, Ruby, and my mother.

Ruth spoke gently and kindly as she told the story, out of respect for my mother, I presumed. Her account of things past seemed honest and neutral. Never far from thinking like a case officer, I made a mental note about her objectivity. She would be a reliable source for further discussions. My mother remained quiet during this part of the conversation.

Uncle Raymond said that one day he and my father had traveled to Danville, Kentucky, and had come near the Smith home on Highland Avenue. Explaining himself, Uncle Raymond said, "We wanted to get a look at you when you would have been about two years old."

"Your father never got over you being adopted, and he wanted to know you," Uncle Raymond stressed.

I was tempted to challenge him, but deferred to just listen and accept what he said without comment.

Over the next hour or two, there was a long recounting of the Bullen family history and many photo albums to look at. Much of it became a blur because the only thing that interested me was developing some sense of who my father was and why he had abandoned my mother and me.

As it turned out, my father was something of a "ladies' man" and had at least three other children that he had abandoned and never supported. Uncle Raymond was quick to point out, however, that my father, "could find work quicker than anyone I have ever seen and could do good work, but he just chose a life of rambling."

We were soon joined by the Bullen children, Charles and Alice, who enlivened the conversation tremendously. Both were gregarious and engaging and spoke openly about the good and bad of the family. Both, of course, remembered my father affectionately and were noncritical. Charles and I had been in Vietnam at about the same time, and we both had a great love for hunting and fishing. Alice invited me to her home to fish her farm pond, which she assured me was full of large-mouth bass, my favorite kind of fishing.

As the day came to a close, we said our goodbyes, all warmly hugged and made promises to see one another again soon. As Mother, JoAnn, Penny and I drove away down the long gravel driveway, my mother commented that she did not believe that Raymond and Clarence had ever made any attempt to see me after I had been adopted by the Smiths.

With considerable bitterness in her voice, Mother said, "He never cared about me or you before you were borned (sic) or anytime while I had you. He could have seen you before I ever gave you to the Smiths, but he didn't care to. I don't believe the story."

I questioned the story as well, thinking it was perhaps selfserving, but I could imagine doing something like Uncle Raymond had claimed they did together. It was striking to me that there was no denial by anyone that I was, indeed, Clarence's son. Ruth, in fact, stressed that the one good thing my father had done was never to deny that I was his son. Somehow, this was significant for her.

Over the next years, I learned a great deal about the Bullen family history and spent considerable time researching our ancestry. I made several attempts to contact my half brother, Perry Bullen, who was the son of my father and Ruby, but to no avail. He did not want to meet me. The other surviving brothers, Hugh and Alvin, were not friendly or interested in getting to know me. They communicated through Ruth, who told me, "They would rather forget the whole matter."

Charles and Alice always remained friendly and we enjoyed many an afternoon talking and enjoying each other's families. I never missed an opportunity when visiting Wartburg to fish Alice's pond, which did have a great number of large-mouth bass and crappie.

In two subsequent conversations with Uncle Raymond, I pressed him about my father's motives for abandoning my mother and me, but he was never quite able to explain how or why my father had left us.

He said, "Your father was a good man, but he liked the ladies too much and could not stay at home. It was just his way."

My efforts to shake his story about coming to Danville to see me were never successful. Uncle Raymond, over many years, steadfastly stuck to his story. He claimed that both he and my father had hoped that I might have been outside playing or being walked by my adopting mother. He insisted they spent a good hour or so just hanging around in the hopes that I would be brought out of the house.

In recent years, there have been a number of deaths in the Bullen family to include Uncle Raymond, his son Colin and daughter Alice. I have seen no real purpose in continuing a relationship with the Bullen extended family since those deaths. So many years have passed as to make our mutual history uninteresting and unimportant to the younger Bullen clan.

13 ▦

Consequences

During the initial two days Penny and I spent with Wynetta and my newfound family, she kept asking me where Yuma Smith was during all of our discussions. I did not talk about Yuma Smith as my mother in any significant way. Penny wanted to know what had happened to the Smiths, accusing me of avoiding any discussion of John and Yuma Smith. Her accusations made me angry because she pressed the theme almost every minute we were alone. Only exhaustion quieted her. In truth, Penny was partially correct about my reticence to discuss the Smiths, but the task at hand was to learn all that we could about my biological origins.

I was acting like the CIA Operations Officer I was, collecting information and putting the puzzle together as quickly as I could. We did not have a lot of time, and an in-depth analysis could be done later.

I also sensed that Penny had taken an immediate dislike to my mother. When we were alone, she would assert that my mother was concerned only with her own story, and her version of the story. Penny also felt it was implausible that my biological mother had given me up to the Smiths for the reasons she claimed. She repeatedly said that there were no circumstances in my mother's story that would warrant giving me away to the Smiths. She based her feelings on the fact that my biological mother was thirty-three years old at the time I was born, a mature woman with some sense of responsibility. Penny found my mother's explanations of marital hardship and abandonment by my father unacceptable.

There was another situation under way, which I did not realize until much later. Penny and I had been married for ten years, and the focus of all of our family activities, vacations and holidays up until then had been with her family in Pittsburgh. We saw my brother David only occasionally. All of a sudden, she now had my mother and three sisters-in-law, and fifty-some other relatives with whom to deal. They had a claim, and they were staking that claim. They wanted to be part of us and wanted us to be part of them. It took some time to sort out this tension.

Penny was not always gentle in how she judged my biological mother's actions and decisions surrounding the adoption. She was openly critical, telling Wynetta that there was no excuse, whatsoever, for abandoning four children. Mother seemed to accept her anger and criticisms. She said that she understood Penny's feelings because Penny was a mother and could never conceive of anything that would force her to give up our two daughters. Mother stressed, however, that her circumstances were different in a different time.

"Things were far less simple," Mother would claim.

Mother saw leaving my sisters with their father and grandmother in a safe environment with extended family that loved them as not such a terrible thing to do. According to Wynetta, there were no circumstances that would compel her to return to Reuben, so leaving the girls was her only choice. One thing was certain at the time of my birth: she was alone and that aloneness accelerated her decision to give me up to the Smiths.

No knowledgeable family member disputes that Mother's husband, Reuben, was a difficult man to live with; however, my sisters and their aunt dispute how Mother took care of her responsibilities on the farm and also her criticisms of the girls' grandmother.

Only my oldest sister, JoAnn, has a vivid recollection of Mother during those years. She was five at the time Mother left the farm in Wartburg. My sister Bobbie was four, and the youngest, Betty, was two and a half. Mother left, and may have periodically visited, but remained essentially gone from the Wartburg farm until Bobbie graduated from high school some fifteen years later.

Mother left the farm to work at Y-12 in Oakridge, Tennessee and soon found herself pregnant.

Once Clarence Bullen learned Mother was pregnant, he left town, leaving her behind to deal with the pregnancy. Mother said she was devastated that Bullen abandoned her, but quickly realized she was completely on her own and would have to make the best of her circumstances. Penny remained dubious.

In my judgment, the truth of the matter was that Mother was completely incapable of taking care of anyone except herself. She did not have the emotional maturity and strength to endure hardship.

Mother was the product of an abusive upbringing and broken relationships that crippled her ability to get outside of herself. She had an absolute need to protect herself from harm, whether it was physical, emotional or spiritual harm.

Over the thirty years I had with her, mother spoke of it many times. When recounting her life and pattern of resolving conflict, she would always say, "When things got to an intolerable place, I simply walked away."

It was her pattern, her salvation, to move on, to get away from the pain.

14 ⵌ

The Bureau

What do the Roman Catholic Church, the Mafia and the FBI have in common?

First, it begins with the leadership. The pope sits on the throne of St. Peter as the absolute undisputed authority of the Roman Catholic Church. The Mafia families are organized in a similar way with absolute power consolidated in a single family head known as the Godfather or *capo* or *capo di tutti* (boss of bosses). The FBI's enormous power is exercised by the director. These are powerful men whose influence is global, going far beyond their immediate realms.

The pope is thought to be, under certain circumstances, infallible. A Mafia boss is never thought of as infallible, but he typically acts with such resolve and finality it makes him appear, at least to some, to be infallible. FBI directors are not infallible, as history has shown, and they act governed by the written and unwritten rules, regulations and laws of our nation, but always from a position of tremendous power and strength. Traditionally all three have resources, in terms of personnel and money, beyond the average person's imagining.

The pope is surrounded by trusted cardinals, bishops and other clerics. The Mafia boss surrounds himself with trusted "made" members. The FBI director is surrounded by a deputy director and 10 or 12 assistant directors. In all three instances, these people surrounding their leaders are "the palace guard." From their seats in Rome, New York and Washington, D.C., they control their underlings by placing other loyal, trusted colleagues in territories or jurisdictions under their control. For example, the pontiff's power is exercised through other bishops who generally control territory, i.e., the Cardinal Archbishop of New York, or the Bishop of Omaha.

The Mafia controls its territories similarly. For example, the Gambino Family has controlled New York for decades. The FBI is organized in a similar manner. There are approximately 52 FBI divisions roughly divided along geographic lines and headed up by a Special Agent in Charge (SAC). Ironically, the basic organizational construct for all three is based on the Roman Legion, which, at the lowest level, numbered 12 soldiers. Other icons to be remembered in this context are the 12 tribes of Israel and the 12 disciples of Christ. Coincidence or not, there is a significance to this imagery for the men who built these organizations from the ground up. Traditional FBI squads numbered about twelve, although today those numbers have grown exponentially.

The Roman Catholic Church is structured in a hierarchical and paternalistic manner. Management, if we can call it that, is responsive and streamlined. The distance from priest to pope is relatively short. A wayward priest comes to the attention of his bishop in very short order and the next stop is Rome. The Mafia also has this short span of control. The distance from a soldier to a *capo* can be only one stop or perhaps two, if a lieutenant sits between the soldier and a *capo*.

In its earliest configuration under Director J. Edgar Hoover, the FBI Agent was responsible to a supervisor who was, in turn, responsible to an Assistant Special Agent in Charge (ASAC), and then to the SAC, who controlled the field division. An FBI Agent who in some manner acted improperly, embarrassing the bureau in some public way especially, would come to the attention of the director in Washington very quickly.

Under Director Hoover and for some years after his death, punishment was swift. Volumes have been written about agents being exiled to undesirable posts such as Butte, Montana, or suspended without pay for weeks, "put on the bricks," as it is known, for a range of infractions or mishaps.

The Church, the Mafia and the Bureau are held together and motivated by personal loyalty to the organization and loyalty to your colleagues, especially to the ones you become associated with early on in your career. The work or mission is vocational, a higher calling to something special, rather than just a job. All three institutions are elitist, requiring unique backgrounds and education, specialized training and rigorous discipline to the rules, written and unwritten.

All three cultures have an "us and them" mentality, which is derived from "secret knowledge" or "insight...." secular Gnostics if you will. These are secretive organizations by nature, all for logical, common sense reasons associated with some of their functions, but they can become perverse and used for covering up abuses. Of course, the Mafia has its clear need for secrecy and is not concerned about abuse.

The Roman Catholic Church and the Mafia remain exclusively

boys' clubs, while the FBI swore in female agents around the time of Hoover's death in 1972. This fact notwithstanding, all three organizations traditionally have "taken care of their own" with respect to promotions, internal investigations and discipline. Some of this has begun to erode in recent years because of public exposure of abuses and demands for more transparency, especially in the cases of the church and FBI. The FBI finally had to succumb to the power of the Inspector General's Office which is now authorized to investigate the FBI's alleged transgressions. In some instances even the Mafia has become concerned about its public image and has sought to clean up its act.

There is a real sense of family in all three, although the "FBI family" is not as closely knit as it once was. During the Hoover era and twenty years beyond, it was common to hear phrases like: "the FBI family," or "he or she is one of us," or "he or she is a good guy." The Mafia uses the same code language. They are part of the family, something larger than themselves. The Mafia began with families and, to some extent, remains so even though there are now more blends of families and alliances that would not have existed in the past. The Roman Catholic Church has its families within the larger family organized as Jesuits, Dominicans, and so forth. Each of these family units has a father figure in the person of the SAC, a *capo*, or an abbot, or father superior, to ensure that the rules and the culture are observed or lived out.

*****

This was the FBI I wanted to be a part of, but it was not to be when I first applied in 1971. When I was qualified to become an FBI Agent, the testing completed and I applied, there was a hiring freeze in place. The SAC of the Washington Field Office told me candidly,

"I would like to hire you, but I cannot. If you were black, a woman, or an accountant, I could hire you today." He said that he thought that it would be six months to a year before my application could be considered, but he advised me to keep my application on file and active in the event the freeze was lifted. I left his office deflated and unhappy.

I decided to apply for positions with the CIA and the State Department. Both began to process my application and sent me for extensive testing and physical examinations. In a manner of weeks, I received an offer from the State Department to work in its overseas security division. I was not terribly interested in this position and asked the CIA recruiters to advance my application since I had an offer on the table. Fortunately, testing had gone well and there was only the hurdle of a polygraph to complete the agency's requirements. Within a matter of days, things happened. I passed the polygraph examination and about ten days later I was offered a position as a staff career trainee. I am certain things went well with the CIA because of work I had done with them in Vietnam. So, my career with the CIA began, and over the years, I would get a postcard from the FBI asking if I wished my application to remain active and on file. I always responded affirmatively.

Eight years later, the FBI made inquiries among my friends and relatives as to my whereabouts. My Aunt Mayme, working at the Pentagon, wrote to me.

My dear Aunt Mayme, never quite certain as to what I was up to, began her letter with the question, "What in the world have you done now? The FBI is looking for you. What should I tell them?" I telephoned her immediately and she told me an FBI Agent had come to her office to inquire as to my whereabouts. He told her, "The FBI might be interested in hiring your nephew." I asked her to call the agent and tell him that I was working in Europe. She could give him my phone number and address without fear.

From my seventh-floor office, I went to the legal attache's office, staffed by a senior FBI Agent, Jerry Grimes. I told Jerry the story. He promised to call FBIHQ and inquire as to their interest. I returned to my office to await word from him. Sometime after lunch, Jerry called me into his office and told me that, indeed, the FBI was interested in hiring me, chiefly because of my fluent Spanish and experience working against hard targets such as the Cubans and Soviets. He said the FBI's Miami Division had come across my application and were interested in having me come on board. They had done some homework and knew my background.

I told Penny that evening. She was ecstatic about the prospects of going home and my becoming an FBI Agent. Her only condition was that there be no more undercover work. The next morning after a long discussion with Jerry about the pros and cons of leaving the CIA and joining the FBI, I told him to advise FBIHQ I would be interested in making a change.

It took some weeks to update an application and complete yet another background investigation. All of this activity required me to officially notify the CIA of my intentions. My immediate supervisor and the station chief were appalled. It was as if I had committed some sort of treasonous act. There had always been competition and mutual disdain between the FBI and the CIA, even though their missions in those days had very little to do with one another.

Nevertheless, the unpleasantries in Europe did not influence CIA Headquarters because they cooperated and transferred me back

to Washington in a routine fashion. After two weeks at CIA Headquarters, I resigned and the following day, January 22, 1979, I was
sworn in as a Special Agent in a ceremony at Quantico, Virginia. It
was the proudest day in my professional life. New Agents' training
lasted sixteen weeks and upon graduation, Penny, Amy and our new-
born daughter, Meghan, and I made our way to Cleveland, Ohio.

Cleveland

The SAC told me not to unpack my bags since I would be
moving to Miami Division after a year of training. I worked bank
robberies and fugitives for the first year in Cleveland. No call came
from Miami. I then was moved to an organized-crime squad. Cleveland Division was a major office with huge criminal and security
programs and some 180 Agents covering all of northern Ohio. The
workload was heavy because crime was unabated and driven largely
by the Licavoli Mafia family, motorcycle gangs and corruption.

Living in Cleveland was very good in spite of stories about the
polluted Cuyahoga River, frigid winters and bad inner city schools.
We loved our modest home in Rocky River and the girls adapted
quickly to their surroundings and new friends. Penny's family was
in near-by Pittsburgh and we saw them as often as we wanted or
needed. As it happened, the Miami Division forgot about me and I
continued to work criminal cases. Life was very good.

A year later I had become the lead investigator for a large ar-
son-for-profit case centered in what is known as the near Westside. .
Bank robberies and fugitives were the last thing on my mind as I
walked into Citizen's Federal Savings and Loan on East Sixth Street
on my lunch break to cash a check. This was long before electronic

banking was available and banks were crowded at noon, and this day was no exception. I was the fourth or fifth person waiting in line to cash a check.

In the line to my left, I noticed a bank employee approach a man who was having some discussion with the teller. In an instant, the banker fell to the floor, after being hit on the jaw by a round-house punch. Still, he held onto the other man, who broke to run for the main entrance, a large, steel-framed glass revolving door. I quickly pulled my credentials and badge from my coat pocket, held them high and announced, "FBI, stop," and chased the subject and the employee, who would not let go of his assailant.

As the subject finally broke loose and entered the revolving door, I somehow found my foot in the jamb, stopping him in his tracks with a hard thump to his forehead as his forward momentum abruptly ended. He was trapped in the triangular space of the door, which was now his cage. As the bank employee moved away from us, he told me that the man had given the teller a "demand note," and she had given him several hundred dollars.

A silent alarm had been sent a few minutes earlier and I could hear police sirens wailing at a distance but growing ever closer. An automatic security gate had come down, closing the entrance, and trapping the two of us with our backs to a throng of amazed witnesses. The captured, angry, dark-eyed man demanded to be let out of his trap. I told him he was not going anywhere. I identified myself as an FBI Agent and told him that he was under arrest for attempted bank robbery. He insisted he had not done anything.

I asked, "What is your name?"

"Bob."

"Bob what?" I insisted.

"Bob Miner."

And then I asked, "What kind of work do you do?"

"I'm in construction and a painter."

I kept going. "Where do you work?"

"I'm unemployed."

"What were you doing in the bank?"

"Nothing," he said, with frustration and a big push on the door, which pinched my foot hard.

I asked Miner, "Do you hear the sirens coming toward us?" And he said that he did. I told him that the police would arrive soon.

"Do you have a gun?" I asked, looking directly at the green windbreaker wrapped around his right hand. He said he did not. I told him to point his hand away and down towards the floor and to unwrap the windbreaker.

I asked again, "Are you sure you do not have a gun?" I told Miner to look outside at the street. Outside the chain-linked security gate two Cleveland police officers were leaning over the hood of their squad car with their shotguns aimed at us. I told Miner that if he did have a gun and he made any quick move we both would likely die where we stood. He repeated he did not have a gun and he unwrapped the windbreaker from around his right hand to show us it was empty.

A Cleveland city police sergeant approached from the rear of the bank with his weapon drawn. I held my credentials and badge high so he could clearly see them, announcing "FBI," while keeping my eyes on Miner, as he fretted over his dilemma. I told the sergeant to tell his officers to stand down and we would remove Miner from the door.

The sergeant and I took Miner from his revolving-door trap, handcuffed him quickly and searched him for weapons, evidence and identification. Finding $514 in the left front pocket of his blue jeans, we moved to an office at the back of the bank and sat him down. I told Miner again he was under arrest and gave him a Miranda warning.

I telephoned the bank robbery supervisor and told him what had happened. He told me to release Miner to the custody of the Cleveland Police Department since Miner was unarmed, no shots were fired and there were no serious injuries. He said his squad, which was on their way to the bank, would interview the bank employees and witnesses. As soon as the bank robbery squad members arrived, I briefed them and left. As I walked back towards the office, I was hungry and wanted to get something to eat, but I did not have any money because I had not cashed the check I had gone to cash.

News of the unique capture of Miner spread quickly in the office and to the media. I received both congratulations and some ribbing about the revolving door incident. The media was amused and lines by the radio broadcasters were real tongue-in-cheek stuff: "Talk about being in the wrong place at the wrong time. Wow! Trying to rob a bank with an FBI Agent there." Miner had to have suffered some kidding of his own in his cell at the county jail.

The case of Robert Miner was typical of the kind of desperation some people were driven to as employment waxed and waned in Cleveland's blue-collar economy. I never saw Miner again because he pled guilty and there was no trial. He was a first-time offender with no criminal record, and he received what I thought was a very stiff sentence of seven to twenty-five years. I was struck by this sentence because white-collar crime defendants stealing way more than Robert Miner could ever conceive of robbing, routinely received much lighter sentences and were often sent to minimum-security prisons.

Little did I know at the time, these kinds of disparities, factored with corruption, politics and other obstacles began to seed in me a great deal of cynicism about our criminal justice system. Yet, that cynicism grew into a more determined and sustained commitment to work all the harder.

*****

In 1982, Cleveland SAC Joe Griffin, attending a meeting in Washington, telephoned me from FBIHQ: "Who the hell have you been talking to?"

Not recognizing his voice or expecting a phone call from the SAC himself, I retorted, "Who the hell is this?"

With considerable emphasis he replied, "Your SAC!"

Meekly, I said, "Yes, sir. What can I do for you?"

Griffin said, "I have just been informed by SAC Dick Held that you are to be reassigned to San Juan, Puerto Rico. Held has authority from the director to draft Spanish speakers with criminal experience to build a new staff in Puerto Rico. Have you told anyone that you are willing to go to Puerto Rico?"

"No, sir," came my quick reply.

Griffin said, "The work you've been doing for the arson program is too important for you to leave now. I do not think I can buy much time with that argument, so we have to think of something else. Go see the ASAC and tell him what is happening, and we will talk later."

I was stunned by this news and quickly found my way to the ASAC's office to discuss this news. ASAC Phillip Urick was a "good guy" and knew the bureau system very well. After considerable discussion, Urick suggested that, because I had an expressed interest in becoming a supervisor, it was imperative I apply for a supervisory position at FBIHQ immediately. He reasoned that, because this was an opportunity for advancement, Held's intention to draft me for a lateral transfer could be thwarted.

After discussing this idea with SAC Griffin, we all agreed on the strategy. I immediately applied for a supervisor's position in the Organized Crime Section at FBIHQ. The plan worked. I was selected for the position and transferred to FBIHQ about ninety days later. This was my first real lesson in understanding how things got done among the men who held the Hoover legacy and still worked it to their advantage.

We had been in Cleveland nearly four years. My wife and children were very happy and settled in Rocky River, Ohio. Our church and school were in the neighborhood. The girls had lots of friends and life was good. Penny's family lived in Pittsburgh, and it was just the right distance for them and us to maintain cordial and festive holidays and contact as needed. She was saddened and angry that I had been forced to leave what was our "happy home."

We were not strangers to Washington and had many friends

there, but we had homesteaded, and neither of us really wanted to leave Cleveland. Penny cried for almost two days as we packed up our things in our lovely center-hall colonial home. In some respects I don't think she ever forgave me for this move.

Washington

Life at FBIHQ was routine in its daily grind, beginning at about 7:15 a.m. Monday through Friday. Our work was essentially to oversee field division programs and operations, giving approvals when and where necessary, and trying to facilitate their logistical and personnel meetings. My days were filled with budget requests, training schedules and briefings up and down the chain of command. I realized this was a necessary stepping stone to another field assignment and as such was a necessary evil to be endured. It is true that some made their careers in Washington, but the majority of us were looking to leave within weeks of first arriving there. Eighteen months passed quickly and I was reassigned to El Paso, Texas, as the FBI supervisor at the El Paso Intelligence Center (EPIC).

El Paso

I thought I had died and gone to Heaven upon our arrival in El Paso. A familiar Mexican and Indian culture so dominated everything from food to architecture, I was euphoric. I remember telling Penny we had all of the advantages of living in the United States but it was like living in Mexico again. We adapted quickly, and the girls made friends at school and church and became avid swimmers and horseback riders.

Work for me was good but complex because I was not responsible to the SAC of the El Paso Division but, rather, to FBIHQ, which had the oversight of EPIC. As time passed, however, I did get involved in some operational matters run by the FBI's El Paso Division. This was a function of my longtime friendship with the SAC I had previously worked for in Cleveland and my interest in case work. It was always more fun and interesting to be on the street working cases than sitting behind a desk.

The Drug Enforcement Agency (DEA) and the United States Customs Service had established the rudimentary beginnings of a centralized intelligence clearinghouse and interdiction center. The premise was that the cooperating agencies such as U.S. Border Patrol, the Bureau of Alcohol, Tobacco and Firearms, et cetera, would provide raw intelligence to EPIC analysts, who in turn would link other bits and pieces of intelligence, fuse the material and report it back out to the field for an interdiction to be made by the appropriate enforcement agency. The natural tensions and concerns for protecting sources was a huge stumbling block and getting our respective organizations to cooperate was a formidable task.

This was a noble effort, and I was committed to the idea, but I was soon frustrated by what seemed to be an unbreakable distrust between the two most critical agencies, my own, the FBI, and DEA. The FBI was new to the enforcement of drug laws, having just taken on concurrent jurisdiction with DEA in 1982, and they thought us to be amateurs; in truth, we were, in some regards. However, there was no agency better at putting together racketeering cases, because of our experience with the Mafia and the RICO statute, (racketeering, influence and corrupt organizations).

In these early years of trying to work together, DEA taught the FBI a great deal about enforcement on the street, but we excelled in bringing the bigger conspiracy cases to fruition. My personal strategy was to be cooperative and accurate in relaying the FBI's position in any operational or policy dispute. It was critical for my own success to remain absolutely loyal to FBI managers and field office personnel, but I had to gain the trust of the other cooperating agencies at EPIC. In truth, it was actually easily done, because I made a conscious decision to be cooperative and open to new strategies for sharing intelligence.

My work at EPIC was essentially staff work and, therefore, was reasonably predictable with respect to schedules and family time. We enjoyed the high desert, culture and our frequent weekend travels to northern New Mexico. We fell in love with Ruidoso, the Albuquerque Balloon Festival and particularly Santa Fe. My daughters and I rode horseback two or three times a week, and Amy became quite the horsewoman, winning ribbons in several of the local competitions in hunter-jumper class. I always thought it a bid odd that we were training and riding English style in what was essentially the Old West of Billy the Kid and Pat Garrett fame.

Early on, we began attending St. Francis on the Hill Episcopal Church, and I became active in prayer groups and the study program known as Education for Ministry (EFM). These activities were incredibly exciting for me, and I threw myself into learning as much as I could about Anglicanism and its U.S. counterpart, the Episcopal Church.

Although I had left the Roman Catholic Church while we were in Central America, this was the first time I really began to understand the Episcopal Church and its traditional roots. This was a period of great personal growth and what I believe to be a time of special grace.

I had told the rector of St. Francis on the Hill something of my background with the Trappists and he asked me to talk about contemplative prayer during a Sunday morning forum. At the conclusion of the talk, a woman approached me and asked why I was not a priest.

In an almost off-handed manner, I replied, "I tried that once and failed." And she then gently said, "Well, perhaps you should try again. The love you have for the religious life was evident this morning. You were beaming."

I didn't give much consideration to her comments until sometime later during an EFM session. The facilitator, an ordained deacon, asked me to stay after class for some private time.

Our conversation began with her question: "Why are you not a priest?" Again, I replied, "I tried that once and failed."

She said, "That was a different time and a different place. You are now in a different tradition and your religious life has matured. It is obvious that God is calling you to ordained ministry. Others in our group have spoken to me about it, and they have the same question: Why are you not a priest?"

I had no answer. I left the meeting flattered, after a fashion, but puzzled as to how people were discerning a call to ministry for me, a full-time, fully committed career FBI Agent. I decided to continue the conversation with our facilitator and other clergy I had met in El Paso. It was about this time that I was named to the newly formed diocesan Hispanic Commission. The purpose of the commission was to develop new ways of bringing Hispanics into the Episcopal Church.

One of the members of this commission was the Reverend Arthur Bevins. Art was a former Roman Catholic priest who had left the church to marry a nurse he had met while he was at the University of Ohio. An intellectual with a keen sense of history, ethics and social justice, he was a formidable debater and advocate for the poor and disenfranchised. As unlikely as it may seem, we became fast friends.

During the 1960s, when he was protesting Vietnam and philosophically aligned with anti-government activities, I was killing Viet Cong and living out what I thought was my duty as a citizen soldier. Art had been radicalized by the deaths of President Kennedy, Bobby Kennedy and Martin Luther King, as well as the war, which he thought was completely inane and anti-human.

He was fond of telling me, "For an FBI Agent, you're not a bad guy. We might just be able to convert you into a real stinking liberal." Of course, his tongue was in his cheek each and every time he made fun of our differences.

It was not long before Art began to talk to me about becoming a priest. I was now better prepared for the discussion because I had done some research about the ordained orders, namely deacon, priest and bishop. Because of my career in the FBI, now into its tenth year, it made no sense to go to seminary and start a new career.

I had indeed broached the subject with Penny, who had reacted fiercely with an unequivocal: "No damn way!" Penny had harbored bad feelings towards the church because, in her view, it had failed her family when her father was dying.

For Art, the answer was easy. I was to go to the diocesan Preacher Lewis School of Ministry to study for the diaconate. It was a three-year program designed to train lay people in church history, theology and liturgics, for ordination as a non-stipendiary (not paid) deacon. The Diocese of the Rio Grande had an exceptionally good program for deacons and used deacons extensively in the vast territory covered by the diocese, namely all of New Mexico and a large section of west Texas, including El Paso.

Penny was distraught at this prospect but decided to give up the fight. I began the school, which met one weekend a month to review assignments and work done in the local parish, under the supervision of the parish priest. In this instance, it was Art, because we had transferred to his parish, St. Christopher's, in the lower valley. St. Christopher's was situated about a thousand meters from the U.S.-Mexican border and was once the home for many Anglo farming families that populated the lower valley. However, the congregation had grown old and many had died off, and we were now surrounded by newly arriving immigrants, principally from Mexico and a few others from Central America. Many were illegal and Art was involved in a sanctuary movement to assist these illegals in leaving the border area for places further north.

As a federal agent, I was put in a delicate position by Art's illegal activities. One afternoon, he asked me what I would do if a hungry Mexican family appeared at the church door and asked for assistance.

I said, "It would depend on what kind of assistance. If they asked for food and clothing, I would provide it from our food pantry and clothing bank and send them on their way, with no further inquiry. On the other hand, if someone came to the door and asked for money and told me they were illegal, I would be forced to refuse and send them on their way."

Art asked, "Would you arrest them?" to which I said, "No. It is not my job as an FBI Agent."

On that day, we came to an easy accord. Art promised never to tell me about his involvement in the sanctuary movement and he agreed never to ask me to assist in any way. I agreed to simply turn away anyone I thought to be illegal without taking any further action. As things turned out, to my knowledge no illegals came to St. Christopher's asking for assistance while I was there for services, meetings or other reasons.

On January 8, 1988, I was ordained a deacon by the Right Reverend William Davidson, Interim Pastoral Bishop. Similar to the days on which my two daughters were born, my ordination felt to me as a "rebirth." It was akin to the notion or sensation of being on the mountaintop in some euphoric fog that God made especially for me. Warned by my friends and colleagues that this state of almost ecstasy would end, I prayed it would not.

Soon, Art had me preaching once a month, helping with the food pantry and building a relationship with county social services. Social services was trying to find a way to help the homeless who had begun to flood El Paso as a result of the Reagan-Bush decision to cut federal funding to state mental institutions. This action caused Texas institutions to turn out many of their patients, who, in many instances, were severely disabled by long confinement, chemically induced palsy and unresolved mental illness, to fend for themselves on Social Security benefits.

In theory, those turned out were to go to metropolitan centers, hook up with Social Security and county services and reintegrate into the communities they chose. The flaw was that most of the folks we encountered sleeping in drain culverts, under cars and in ditches were completely incapable of handling their affairs. They were truly lost. Members of our congregation would search these folks out and try to persuade them to come to our now-established sanctuary known as Las Palmas, a partially rehabbed, very old motel.

My job was to find financial support and the physicians who could assist in the care of our residents. I soon got a reputation for begging, extorting and cajoling every person of means in El Paso for assistance to Las Palmas. Soon, many of my friends were running away from me. Nonetheless, this was the traditional servanthood work of a deacon, taking care of the poor and marginalized. This was the ministry to which I knew God had called me. In it all, I became quite radicalized and a strong advocate for the poor we encountered in El Paso. I had begun to see people in a different light. I was now less suspicious and cynical, and certainly more willing to entertain people's stories of hardship and personal deprivation.

*****

My FBI responsibilities continued normally, and on one incredibly hot afternoon in downtown El Paso I was the supervisor of a drug surveillance. One of the subjects decided to get a haircut and entered a shop just off Main Street. The surveillance team, consisting of four people on foot and a couple of others in vehicles, took up various positions. The lead surveillance agent was a woman with limited experience. From my vantage point in the van, I noticed a bag lady pushing an old shopping cart coming directly toward the agent as she tried to remain inconspicuous yet keep an eye on the subject. A conversation ensued and before I knew it the agent had taken the hand of the bag woman and walked her into the coffee shop, breaking off her vantage point on the subject.

I was astounded. In a few minutes, the agent and the bag lady reappeared on the street, chatting amiably. The bag lady now had food and something to drink. She hugged the agent, took up her cart and walked on down the way. The agent resumed her eyeball position on the subject, and we resumed the surveillance without further interruption. By the end of the shift, I was both curious and angry with this First Office Agent (FOA). Rather than make an issue about breaking off the surveillance in front of the other agents, I asked to meet at a local bar for a debriefing.

"What the hell were you doing? You had the eye on the subject and you broke off the surveillance, jeopardizing the entire operation. Why did you talk to this bag lady?"

The FOA calmly said, "She needed something to eat, so I took a few minutes to get her some food."

"It is not your job to feed the poor. You were the lead on this surveillance and you jeopardized it. Why did you feel compelled to help this woman?"

Her answer was, simply, "As I watched the woman come toward me, I thought: but for the grace of God there go I. So I helped her."

Our conversation ended. There was nothing more to be said. I recognized this as one of God's moments. The Irish would call it being in or experiencing "thin time." This moment accentuated for me and caused me to focus on the duality of my life... one foot firmly planted in the religious life and the other living in the harsh realities of the underbelly of our society. Both demanded my full attention and commitment; failure in either could cause me to lose my life... for eternity.

Minneapolis

In 1988, I applied for a field supervisory position in Minneapolis Division and ultimately was selected for the job. In July 1988, we drove from El Paso to Minneapolis over three days, arriving on the Fourth of July in a heat wave of 95 degrees. I wondered what in the world I had done. It was hotter in Minneapolis than the high desert of El Paso, which we had left in the 80-degree range. We went about our normal finding of temporary quarters, getting oriented to the city, locating schools for the girls and beginning to search the real estate market.

We found Minneapolis pleasant enough but strikingly different from the culture we had come from. Minnesotans, we soon discovered, have a "you are not from here" mentality. We ended up buying a lovely new home in Lakeville, some distance from downtown Minneapolis, where the FBI office was located. Minneapolis Division covered Minnesota, North and South Dakota.

I soon discovered that I had inherited "a rubber gun squad" that was content with running background investigations, spending time in the gymnasium and giving lip service to our designated work in the Government Crimes Program (GCP), which should have been producing many more arrests, indictments and convictions. I also found that my direct and abrupt style did not go well with the agents who were comfortable in their homes. Many of them were native Minnesotans.

No one on my squad in Minneapolis, with two exceptions, was interested in doing any hard work. I was responsible for the GCP which was the main work for the division agents centered mostly in the Dakotas. I also had direct line authority over the resident agencies in North Dakota.

Another agent supervisor handled South Dakota. All agents assigned to the Dakotas were principally involved in the GCP, which was dedicated to investigations of violent crimes on the Indian reservations in their territories. These felony cases were numerous and often difficult because of the terrific level of violence among the Indians. Typically we carried 300 open violent crime investigations annually in the Dakotas.

Our farthest outpost was the Minot, North Dakota Resident Agency, a 600-mile plane trip from Minneapolis. We referred to our work on the reservations as "Indian fighting."

This work was incredibly dangerous, with the ever present threat of violence and the extreme weather conditions that plagued our winters. It was not uncommon for agents to conduct investigations and make arrests in temperatures twenty and thirty degrees below zero. In these conditions, having a car break down or having an accident, with a prisoner in tow, was my greatest nightmare. The distances resident agents traveled from their offices to the various reservations were great. One could easily travel for miles and never see another car. The population of North Dakota at the time was less than 200,000... and as James Michener wrote in his book *Centennial*: "The Great Plains of the Dakotas are not fit for human habitation and should be populated only by buffalo and nomadic Indian tribes..." That more than adequately describes the isolation one experiences there.

My first year in the division was miserable. I would leave for the office at 4:30 in the morning to read and review files, meet with the ASAC and SAC, and answer inquiries about cases and investigations, as well as monitor the activities of my agents in Minneapolis and North Dakota. I traveled one week each month to North Dakota to review and supervise the work of the agents there.

The SAC was unsympathetic about the shortcomings of the agents assigned to my squad in Minneapolis and demanded that they produce or, as he put it, "I will find a supervisor who can motivate these people. Their success or failure is your success or failure, and if you do not get these people to work you will no longer be an FBI supervisor."

I knew the SAC's reputation, and he meant what he said. I, therefore, began to search for new blood to invigorate the squad, shifting the non-producers to other squads in the office. This took some time, but, to my surprise, there were three or four ambitious agents who saw an opportunity to excel and liked their chances working on my squad. My plan was simple: If the agents worked hard and successfully brought cases to prosecution, they would receive the best cars, the best training, liberal leave and any other benefit I could bring to them for their efforts. When others in the office began to see this pattern, a number of agents requested to be transferred to my programs.

Over the next three and a half to four years, the agents under my supervision and programs made the most arrests and got the most convictions in the GCP in the history of the FBI. We consistently led all other divisions in our initiation of cases, investigations, prosecutions and convictions during this period.

Our child sexual abuse caseload and program was nationally recognized as innovative and we were determined to eradicate this criminal menace that had infected the Native Americans in the Dakotas. Child sexual abuse was unknown in Native American culture until the isolation of reservation life, poverty and alcohol prevailed. For example, Standing Rock Reservation is ninety miles south of Bismark, North Dakota on a plateau that can only be described as desolate and windblown. The isolation, poverty and alcoholism, and dependence upon government subsidies, have reduced a proud warrior culture to a people turned inward, bringing violence on themselves. Most regrettably, it is the children who suffer the most.

The resident agents assigned to the Dakotas were the most courageous, dedicated and hardest working agents I had ever had under my supervision. I once complained to the SAC that our work got very little notice from Washington, and he asked, "Do you think anyone in Washington gives a damn what we are doing among the Indians? You have to be fighting organized crime or drugs in New York or Chicago to get Washington's attention. The best you can hope for is that you are doing something good and worthwhile for our local communities."

I had always known our SAC to be a tough customer, but now I knew he was a sensitive, very astute hard-ass. I found this new reality to be energizing, causing me to refocus and to work harder at solving these crime problems that plagued the Indians in particular. Little did I know I was being radicalized on social matters once again.

Special Agent David was one of two resident agents in Minot and was responsible for investigations on the Turtle Mountain Indian Reservation. One early afternoon, he was transporting a prisoner from the reservation to Minot for a pretrial hearing. The prisoner had murdered a relative. Bureau procedure required that the prisoner be handcuffed behind the back, placed in the rear of the car and secured by a seatbelt.

David and the prisoner began the trip from Turtle Mountain to Minot at about 11 a.m. It was a clear day, with bright blue skies, persistent winds from the west and some snow on the ground. It was 40 below zero.

An hour into the trip the car stalled. David got out of the car and looked under the hood. Ice had formed a block around the fan, and was sticking to the radiator, rendering the car inoperable. He had no clue how to solve this problem. Getting back into the car, he tried to contact the state police by radio, but was out of range.

The prisoner said to David, "We're going to die here if you don't do something." Panic was beginning to set in.

The prisoner said firmly, "Build a fire."

"What?" David asked.

"Build a fire under the fan and the radiator."

"How the hell am I going to do that?"

"Gather some of the smaller twigs and taller grasses from the roadside, put them under the fan and use your notebook paper to set the fire. Get it hot enough, the ice will melt and we can get out of here."

By his own admission, David thought his prisoner was crazy; but, given their circumstances, it was the only thing left to do. He gathered twigs and frozen grass and piled it under the fan and radiator. Somehow he got a fire hot enough to melt the frozen ice from the fan, dropping it onto the fire itself. To his amazement, he was able to start the car and continue the trip.

Some miles down the road, the same thing occurred and he repeated the same procedure. What normally would have been an hour-and-a-half trip took some five hours to complete. They arrived safely at the courthouse and David graciously thanked his murderous prisoner for saving their lives.

I grew to love the work and the agents I supervised in the Minneapolis Division, but my marriage was on the rocks because of my almost exclusive dedication to the job. An additional factor was that often my church life as a deacon took up valuable family time on the weekends. Penny understandably had grown resentful and unhappy. We ended up not talking about the real issues and things fell apart. Once we divorced, Penny and Meghan, the younger of the two girls, moved to Washington, D.C. Amy and I remained in Minneapolis.

*****

As I moved into my fifth year in the division, I grew restless and wanted to transfer back to FBIHQ. Such a move would have likely brought a promotion, and so I began to apply for various positions at FBIHQ. Luckily there was a unique opportunity to go to the National War College for one year of postgraduate study at the Inter-American Defense College (IADC). The focus of IADC was on U.S.-Latin American relations and about fifty percent of the class were senior military and diplomatic officers from Latin America.

I was uniquely qualified because my undergraduate degree was in Latin American studies and I was fluent in Spanish, another requirement. The only drawback to this change was that it was a lateral transfer and I would remain at the same pay level. My transfer orders came in June, and I purposely left immediately after my fifth-year anniversary in Minneapolis, just to mark my longest tour in one place.

Washington

IADC was an extraordinary year of study mixed with travel to important historic sites and military facilities in the United States which enhanced the backgrounds of all of us, but it was particularly beneficial to the Latin American officers. We had personal tours of Gettysburg, for example, by historians who brought places like Little Round Top to life. We toured West Point, the Naval Academy and the Air Force Academy, receiving in-depth briefings by the commandants and other staff.

Among the twenty or so U.S. military officers in the class it was ironic that not one was a veteran of Vietnam. All of these officers were lieutenant colonels or above but a career U.S. diplomat and I were the only two in the class who had served in Vietnam.

A four-country swing through Latin America was a highlight of this year. We began with the Dominican Republic, then had a stopover in Puerto Rico, a longer stay in Venezuela and four days in Colombia. In each instance, we were received by the highest levels of the host governments and had the opportunity to engage in productive exchanges of ideas.

This experience was broadening for me personally and to the benefit of the FBI because of the valuable contacts I made among the U.S. officers at the National War College and the officers from Latin America. Our graduation was in June, and I returned to FBI-HQ where I was assigned to the National Security Division (NSD).

The NSD was about to undergo a significant restructuring of the terrorism section, which was headed up at the time by the famous and infamous John O'Neil. During the preparations for realignment, I was assigned as unit chief for domestic terrorism.

These were heady days with our first major anthrax case, the Freeman movement in Idaho, the proliferation of militia and tragedies such as TWA 800. I found O'Neil to be impossible to work for. We were often at odds as to what were truly matters of urgency or just his proclivity to make a big deal out of every case we had to work. O'Neil loved to "spin up" our Special Operations Center with lots of staff and activity getting the director's attention. The pace was exhausting and I believed it was often unnecessary.

The 1996 Atlanta Olympics

In October 1995, Robert Blitzer was named chief of the Domestic Terrorism Section, and O'Neil remained the chief of the International Terrorism Section. Blitzer made it possible for me to head the new Special Events Management Unit in his new section. This turned out to be an incredible opportunity to establish the FBI as a major player in special events like major athletic series or national political party events requiring law enforcement resources. The dangers of terrorism had dictated that along with other law enforcement, like the United States Secret Service, the FBI would direct and manage security preparations for the 1996 Olympics in Atlanta.

The Atlanta Olympics became the focus of my work. After visiting the FBI's Atlanta Division and other law enforcement there we realized that the security preparations for the Olympics were in real trouble. There was not enough law enforcement in the entire state of Georgia to staff a single 24-hour shift. Another concern was lack of cooperation between various law enforcement agencies within the state. Georgia politics encumbered things greatly. That was not obvious to even an astute observer, and required considerable work to sort out. Things became so difficult at one point that Senator Sam Nunn and Vice President Gore had to weigh in to persuade people to "do the right thing."

My job as unit chief turned out to be finding the funding and the manpower to put into Atlanta's efforts to provide security for all of the venues, athletes and supporting facilities.

Through a series of briefings to United States Attorney General Janet Reno and Deputy Attorney General Jaime Gorlick, I was given the task of keeping the White House apprised of the FBI's activities in Atlanta. This meant frequent meetings with the deputy attorney general and Richard Clark, counterterrorism adviser at the White House. Suffice it to say, these were busy days filled with tension and tremendous effort by many to secure the Olympics. As the FBI weighed in more heavily, cooperation improved among law enforcement in Georgia, and Washington was by and large comfortable with our overall planning.

I was privileged on three occasions to personally brief Vice President Gore, once at FBIHQ, once at the White House and the last time in Atlanta. The vice president was not an easy customer, but he seemed to appreciate my straightforward, candid manner and many of his major concerns were assuaged after our meeting at the White House. It also did not hurt that I was a fellow Tennessean and we had some common experiences to share during the few relaxed moments between briefings.

I was also honored to travel to Rome, Italy, in March 1996, to brief all of the European chiefs of police about security preparations in Atlanta so they would be at ease with the travel of their athletes to the United States. This was a particularly wonderful trip because I was able to take an additional day or two over the weekend and visit the Vatican.

As the start of the Olympics came closer, briefings of Ms. Reno became more frequent. About three weeks before the Olympic opening ceremonies, I was asked to provide Ms. Reno with a detailed briefing as to the overall security preparations. Blitzer and I made our way to Ms. Reno's conference room to be greeted by the deputy attorney general and Ms. Reno's aide.

We took our seats near the head of the large conference table, Blitzer sitting across from me as I sat down in the second chair next to the deputy. We all stood as Ms. Reno entered the room, and she asked us to be seated. The deputy reintroduced Blitzer and me to Ms. Reno and stated the purpose of our meeting. Ms. Reno then asked if I would mind bringing my flip chart closer and sit directly next to her at the head of the table. She simply stated that she was tired, not feeling very well and would like to put her head down on the table as I talked.

I moved to her side, and the deputy scooted down a bit to make room. Ms. Reno put her head down on her forearms and said to me, "Perry, don't worry if I close my eyes. I will be listening." I proceeded with the briefing, which took about forty-five minutes. Ms. Reno was, throughout, engaged and interested, asking penetrating questions as were needed.

At the conclusion of the briefing, Ms. Reno thanked us for the thorough briefing and our patience with her, and asked our forgiveness for her fatigue. I can only remember that I was so impressed by her humility and display of vulnerability that I was speechless and only acknowledged with a nod that she was leaving the room. The deputy thanked us as well for an excellent briefing and departed with Ms. Reno.

The Olympics came and went and the Richard Jewell part of the story is now well known. I was in the FBI Special Operations Center with Director Freeh, the deputy attorney general and others when those fateful decisions were made in an investigation that was to some extent being driven by a media frenzy. I will say only we were not at our best at that time.

My work in NSD had taken me to the highest levels of the United States government and given me a unique exposure and insight to how our policy makers work and what can be done when commitments and planning come together.

The security of the Atlanta Olympics was a monumental task accomplished by extraordinary measures and levels of cooperation never seen before between law enforcement and the United States military. It is essentially unknown that the Third Army provided incredible support to the Olympics in the form of bus drivers, traffic monitors, magnetometer stations and other unarmed logistical support. The FBI itself put some 3,000 personnel in the field. This was probably the greatest unknown federal forces "invasion" of Atlanta since Sherman burned the city in 1864.

Puerto Rico

Almost immediately after the Olympics I was drafted by FBI

Director Freeh to be ASAC, San Juan, Puerto Rico. San Juan Division was considered to be one of the most difficult to staff and to run. A colleague from Atlanta, Rod Beverly, was also selected as ASAC. Rod was to run the drug program, which was a major concern of San Juan Division. The other programs, as well as administration, fell to me.

My immediate chore was to increase the staff from 100 agents to 190. Incentives had to be found to get the kind of agents we wanted, namely, those with significant criminal investigation background and knowledge of Spanish. There were other complications, such as renovating and expanding our space in an old federal building while we continued operations there. That was a farce and ill advised; however, I had no power to change the decision that had been made to do so.

The caseload in San Juan was staggering and complicated because of corruption within the Puerto Rican Police Department. There was no political will to curtail corruption in any of its many forms within the government. The aftermath of hurricanes or tropical storms was fertile ground for abuse of FEMA's largess and lack of control over spending. A tractor or generator which would typically rent in the hundreds of dollars a day would now become hundreds of dollars per hour. City officials often controlled, through their various family members, companies that rented such equipment.

Another problem in Puerto Rico was drug trafficking and its attendant kidnappings and ransoms for deals gone bad or for drugs not paid for. These cases would eat up staff at an incredible rate because of the proclivity for a macho approach to solving a case as quickly as we could, with all of the personnel working at the same time until it was either over or we all dropped from exhaustion. The level of violence in these cases was tremendous and required careful planning with large numbers of agents to ensure safety for ourselves as well as citizens.

The unfortunate reality of Puerto Rico is that it is 1,000 miles south of Miami and of little concern to Washington or anyone else for that matter. I was again confronted with the reality that the only difference the FBI made was in the local community. We were not completely ignored by Director Freeh because he had planned and expected success from the SAC and the two ASACs he assigned there, but beyond that we were basically ignored by Washington.

Without question, it was the hardest assignment in my career, but on some levels, particularly as it pertains to the incredible agents and support staff working in Puerto Rico, it was perhaps some of the best work of my career.

Washington

I was happy to receive my next promotion to the Senior Executive Service and leave Puerto Rico on the anniversary of my two years there. I had not slept a full night in two years and I was exhausted. Little did I know at the time that I had extremely high blood pressure and a blockage of the right coronary artery. These conditions were discovered during a routine physical exam when I returned to FBIHQ and they had to be dealt with immediately.

Returning to Washington was easy and without any major upheaval. My new assignment at Defense Threat Reduction Agency (DTRA) was housed at an office complex adjacent to Dulles Airport. I decided to locate in nearby Reston, Virginia. In doing so, I was about seven minutes from work, twenty minutes from my daughters and forty minutes in to FBI Headquarters.

I reported to work and got a feel for the new director of DTRA, Dr. Jay Davis, a University of California physicist with a flair for the irreverent. We got on well and started some serious thinking about how to better integrate law enforcement and military resources in the event of a national emergency such as World Trade Center 1 in 1993. My briefings before assignment to DTRA at FBIHQ were clear. The World Trade Center was unfinished business, and FBI analysts and others in the intelligence community were certain another attack would come.

My most immediate problem was the medical one, and I began a series of visits with doctors. My blood pressure was out of control, and I had a blockage of the right coronary artery, which required the placement of a stent. I had no idea how ill I had become until the stent opened up the artery. On the morning after, I reported to my doctor I was feeling wonderful and was ready to go home.

He replied, "It's amazing what a little oxygen will do for you." I was back to work within the week. My newfound energy and good spirits amazed me.

Work at DTRA at the senior executive level was an extraordinary time in my life because it gave me the opportunity to travel to the former Soviet Union and support educational efforts by the U.S. government to prevent the proliferation of nuclear materials throughout the world. DTRA held the charter for counterproliferation and the FBI played a key role in supporting those efforts.

I spent considerable time in Budapest, Hungary, working with our school for training former security service people from the Soviet bloc (Czechoslovakia, Armenia, and so on) in counterproliferation strategies. We also provided hand-held detection equipment for many of the officers working in the field examining the cargo containers of trucks and railways.

My first trip to Russia and the Ukraine with Director Davis and a small entourage was perhaps one of the most memorable of my life. We arrived in Moscow for a series of meetings during a very cold November. There was little time to adjust to the time change and the food because of a breakneck schedule visiting the various Russian agencies responsible for nuclear, chemical and biological activities.

It was incredible to be sitting across the table from men who had been our enemies for the entire Cold War, now seeking to remedy the proliferation of WMD. These were the very Russian officers who had their fingers on the buttons of missiles directed toward the United States. Now we were drinking vodka, eating crepes of salmon and caviar and toasting our newfound friendship and alliance. The irony of it all was beyond my imagination.

As a former CIA officer and now senior FBI official, I wondered how I was in this place. My counterparts in the Russian and Ukrainian security services, formerly the KGB and GRU, gave me hints here and there that their dossier on me was quite complete, and they knew why I was part of this mission to their countries.

The head of the Ukrainian security service and I spoke quite openly about our former roles, of course without revealing any secrets, but we did enjoy waltzing down memory lane about our time in our respective clandestine services. He had spent a number of years in the United States, Canada and England early in his career. He was charming and witty, with an excellent command of English.

My time at DTRA also provided me with the opportunity to learn a great deal about our own defense systems. I was privileged to have attended and supported Director Davis in a number of extremely high-level defense panels chaired by the likes of Defense Secretary William Cohen and Deputy Secretary John Hamre. Former CIA Director James Slessinger, and 1958 Nobel Prize for Medicine winner Joshua Lederberg were among the most entertaining in these forums, constantly kibitzing and ribbing each other about their intellectual acumen. However, all ten or twelve men and women who formed these various panels were serious about matters concerning the security of the United States and worked hard on the problems set before them.

One of two primary concerns was related to how best to share and integrate intelligence collected by the many disparate organizations in the United States. The second concern was with interdiction itself or how to stop a terrorist attack before it happened. A number of DTRA entities were conducting independent studies that would model a terrorist incident and try to predict outcomes. Many of these models required testing at various test facilities throughout the country, and I was privileged to witness a number of these tests. My responsibility in all of this was to provide to the Department of Defense the law enforcement perspective and keep FBIHQ apprised as to the work being done at DTRA.

I believe that this seminal work was critical to the FBI security support at the Salt Lake Winter Olympics because we were better able to train and equip the personnel. It is also a certainty that the work done at DTRA better prepared the United States government for our response to 9/11.

The creation of joint intelligence and fusion centers had broken down many of the former barriers of communication and exchanges of intelligence. The chief players, such as the FBI, CIA, NYPD and many others participated fully with confidence that sources and methods now could be effectively protected.

In truth, many obstacles remain and old prejudices die hard, but we have come a long way and the common enemy of terrorism has served to make us better.

About a year out from retirement I began to think about security jobs in the private sector and what I might do after retirement. At this juncture, I had now done over thirty years of intelligence and criminal work. I was not sure I had much more energy for doing what I had already been doing.

*****

In parallel with my time at DTRA, I was functioning as a deacon at the cathedral in Baltimore on Saturdays and Sundays. My ministry there was to visit the homebound, usually on Saturdays, and serve at the altar with the other cathedral clergy on Sundays. I was on the preaching schedule once a month. Once, about a week before I was to preach, I was working on my sermon and had run into some difficulty with the text and the flow of how I wanted to present that particular Gospel. A priest friend invited me to her home on Wednesday to discuss the sermon. We worked on the text for about an hour in her lovely garden in Annapolis.

When we finished the work, Phoebe asked, "When are you going to retire from the FBI?"

"In about six months," I replied.

"And what are you going to do?" she asked.

I told her I was looking for a security job in the private sector. She grew serious and asked, "When is it that you are going to do what God intends for you?"

"And what might that be?" I retorted sarcastically.

Her reply was quick. "God wants you to be a priest, and it is as plain as the nose on your face; but strangely, you either refuse or you cannot see it. Those of us around you see it. You need to go to seminary."

As Phoebe spoke, she outlined presenting my case to the bishop, shopping for a seminary and garnering the various recommendations that would be required. She had thought through her plan; now she was trying to persuade me of its merits.

"You have twenty-four hours to make an appointment with the bishop," she said, "and if you do not I will make it for you. Tomorrow by noon I will check to see if you have done so."

"Yeah, yeah," I replied, and we said our good-byes. I was not unsettled by this idea but I had really not given the priesthood much thought because I had committed to being a deacon, and it was intended to be a life-long commitment. Thursday morning at about five minutes to noon, my private line at the office rang, and I answered, to hear the voice of Phoebe.

"You have not called the bishop. You have five minutes to make an appointment or I will call his office and make it for you."

"Give me a break here, Phoebe. I'm trying to think about what we discussed yesterday, and I am not sure."

"Make the appointment," she said, and she hung up.

I called the bishop's office, and his secretary, Juanita, answered. Upon hearing my voice, she asked, "What is going on with you? The bishop came in here this morning at 8 o'clock asking if I had heard from you lately, and he wondered if you were about to retire from the FBI. Then Phoebe called five minutes ago, asking if you had made an appointment with the bishop. Now I'm talking to you. This is all too much. What is going on?"

I told Juanita that I wanted an appointment with the bishop but there was no hurry, so sometime in the next thirty days would be fine. Juanita said, "As luck would have it, he has a cancellation tomorrow at noon, and you are welcome to come up tomorrow." I agreed.

The bishop and I had a cordial, warm relationship from our work together at the cathedral. As the liturgical deacon for the cathedral, I often served beside him throughout the year. We also knew each other from the Commission on Ministry for the Diocese, which I was a part of. He received me warmly and we chatted easily about my forthcoming retirement. I then switched gears and told him that some of my friends, most especially Phoebe, had raised the prospects of my going to seminary to become a priest. He asked a number of background questions, and once done with those clarifications, the bishop surprised me by saying that he, too, had thought for a very long time that I should consider the priesthood.

Under the Canons of the Church, deacons are solely responsible to their bishop, and he or she can direct or assign deacons with impunity. The bishop decided to use his power and told me to begin to look at several seminaries for the coming fall. We decided that the first obvious choice would be Virginia Theological Seminary (VTS), and the second would be General Seminary in New York.

He also insisted that I look at his alma mater, Episcopal Divinity School at Yale. The die was cast, and I left his office, surprisingly elated, because what we had decided seemed absolutely right, and that sensation gave me a calm that I had not experienced in a very long time.

Soon, I was reviewing catalogues and planning trips to the three seminaries. The decision became a practical one. I had a home in Virginia, my daughters lived in Virginia and in Virginia was a seminary I could afford. Since I was to be retired with a federal pension, there would be no financial assistance coming my way. The bishop had made that point before I left his office. With the bishop's approval and recommendations, I made application to VTS. After some weeks of interviews, interrogatories and other administrative matters, I was accepted at VTS. There was much to accomplish over the next weeks and months.

I submitted paperwork to FBIHQ indicating my intention to retire on August 31, 2001. A retirement ceremony had to be planned and coordinated with DTRA as well as NSD. I sold my house in Reston and moved into off-campus seminary-recommended housing and began to prepare for school beginning in September. As things developed, my retirement ceremony was held at DTRA with some 200 guests attending from the FBI and the defense community.

Various presentations and awards were made, and the NSD assistant director presented my now retired credentials and badge mounted on a very attractive wall plaque. I presented my daughters with gifts of flowers and Teddy bears. My farewell speech was emotional and difficult, but heartfelt.

Most memorable was the master of ceremony, Jim Wright's,

comments pertaining to the question a number of folks had asked, "How in the world does one leave the FBI to become a priest?"

Unknown to me, Wright had given this considerable thought and told the audience that there was nothing unusual about my intention to become a priest because I had already lived a life of service to God and country, and the priesthood would be a continuation of that life. He remarked that it is service to others that is at the core of the work or life of soldiers and FBI Agents and that, to his understanding, service lies at the heart of the priesthood. Wright's perspective in some ways clarified my own reservations and thinking.

G-Man, FBI Special Agent, circa. 1990

THE BISMARCK TRIBUNE

Established in 1873 Thursday, June 15, 1989

William N. Roesgen .... Publisher
Kevin Giles .... Editor
Ted Quanrud .... Editorial Page Editor

OUR VIEW

Finally some really said 'NO' to drugs

A large-scale drug crackdown on North Dakota's Indian reservations has netted 18 arrests so far this week, with FBI authorities anticipating more.

Another tale of social problems on the reservation?

Not entirely. This wasn't your usual "narc-nabs-dealer" story. These drug busts were an example of people taking a stand to improve their communities. That, in fact, is the only way that drug trafficking can ever be stopped.

FBI supervisor J. Perry Smith said the investigation culminating in this week's arrests came about because residents of Fort Berthold and Standing Rock demanded action to stop the drug selling in their communities.

If that sounds only logical, keep in mind that no other North Dakota community has taken such a dramatic stand to recognize drugs as a major problem that needs to be solved.

Drug unit investigators in Bismarck, for instance, will quickly tell you that trafficking is a bigger problem than capital city residents realize. News stories have in fact publicized such comments. But life (and drug sales) go on.

Smith said the arrests should disrupt the flow of marijuana and, to some extent, other drugs onto the two reservations involved.

It's not a total solution, but it is a strong first step.

Those who cared enough about their community and families to demand action on Fort Berthold and Standing Rock are to be congratulated.

May more North Dakotans follow suit.

The Bismark Tribune editorial

THE MINOT DAILY NEWS

Established 1884   Minot, North Dakota, 58701, Wednesday, June 14, 1989   Vol. 74   No. 45

Year-long drug probe results in 12 arrests

By LAURA SWEEP
Daily news Staff Writer

Federal, state and county law enforcement officials pulled in the net Tuesday on a year-long investigation of drug trafficking on the Fort Berthold Indian Reservation.

Twelve persons were arrested and a car and an undisclosed quantity of drugs were confiscated, J. Perry Smith, FBI supervisory special agent for North Dakota, said at a news conference Tuesday.

Those arrested include Joseph "Smoking Joe" Chase, 31; Joseph Iverson, 28; Harlan McCarty, 25; Sherri Schlag, also known as Sherri Vondal, 24; Wilson Starr Jr., 32; Anthony Vondal, 29, all of New Town;

Mary Colfey, 31; Kevin Beston, also known as Kevin McCarty, 24; Tommie McCarty, 37; Rose St. Claire, 28, and Blaine Thomas, 34, all of Minot; and Samuel Meyer Jr., 32, White Shield.

Additional arrests are anticipated, Smith said. The 12 were indicted by a grand jury meeting in

Fargo last week. In addition, two others indicted are fugitives. Officers confiscated an undisclosed amount of drugs and a 1986 Oldsmobile Cutlass 442 belonging to Iverson. The car was confiscated under a federal seizure warrant, Smith said.

The investigation began in response to citizen complaints about drugs, primarily marijuana, on the reservation, Smith said, reading a news release from Jeffrey Jamar, special agent in charge of the Minneapolis division of the FBI, which covers North Dakota, South Dakota and Minnesota.

Tuesday's roundup involved 25 law enforcement officers from the FBI, Bureau of Indian Affairs, state Drug Enforcement Unit, Mountrail and Ward County sheriff's departments and the Minot Police Department.

"This is very much a joint effort," Smith said.

"The focus of our investigation is on the distributors." The drugs were being imported from South Dakota, Montana, New Mexico and Colorado, he said.

See PROBE — Page A5

Smith

(Continued from Page A1)

The investigation involved informants, electronic monitoring, citizens' tips and "all of the resources available to us," Smith said. The investigation is continuing.

Although the 12 arrested were not part of a single drug ring, "I think it's fair to say these people know each other," he said.

U.S. Magistrates Kenneth Knutson, Minot, and Karen Klein, Fargo, worked into the evening Tuesday conducting initial appearances for the defendants at the Federal Courthouse in Minot.

All were released on $2,500 unsecured bond, which means they did not have to post any cash, but will be subject to pay the $2,500 if they fail to make any court appearances.

Knutson indicated arraignments will be scheduled in about 10 days, according to Deputy U.S. District Clerk Candy Schaefer. Assistant U.S. Attorney Cameron Hayden handled the initial appearances, but Assistant U.S. Attorney Clare Hoch-

halter is listed as the attorney of record and may be prosecuting future proceedings, she said.

Minot attorneys appointed by the magistrate to represent the defendants are:

Chase, Gary Lee; Colfey, David Bogue; Harlan McCarty, R. James Maxson; Beston, Michael Ward; Tommie McCarty, Collin Dobrovolny; Meyer, Ed Bosch; Schlag, Steve Farhart; Starr, Todd Cresap; St. Claire, Moody Farhart; Thomas, Richard Hagar; Vondal, Steve Farhart.

Iverson indicated he would retain an attorney, Schaefer said.

The Minot Daily front page after our initial arrests on the reservations.

A light disguise for an undercover operation,
Cleveland, 1979.

For Perry Smith with best wishes,

Al Gore

Credit: Official White House photograph. Briefing Vice President Gore on security planning for the 1996 Atlanta Olympics.

Briefing Vice President Gore at FBI Headquarters, 1996.

Credit: Official Department of Justice photograph. Presenting Attorney General Janet Reno with an FBI Olympic Commemorative Pin. The Deputy Attorney General Jamie Gorelick is to the right. 1996

15 ⌗

Virginia Theological Seminary

Seminary began the next week. On September 11, 2001, eleven days after my retirement from the FBI, I sat reading on a bench in front of the seminary library in what is called "the close."

I heard a terrible noise of a low-flying, fast-approaching aircraft. Hearing the explosion and feeling the ground shake, I was certain the aircraft had missed the runway at Reagan National Airport. Another seminarian approached as he walked by and said, "Perry, I think that plane crashed." I agreed and told him that, from the sound of it, it had crashed short of the runway. Then another student came running from the dormitory, telling us to come to the TV room to watch the events that were unfolding in New York and now in Washington.

My most immediate concern was for my daughters, both of whom were in the Washington metro area, and I wanted them at home with their mother. I eventually spoke to them by telephone, and they made their way home. I left school to ponder what was happening and if there was anything I should do.

Over the next days and weeks, I got tremendous pressure from my then-girlfriend and children to return to the FBI. It was hard for

them to understand that once one retires from the FBI... you are retired! In those days, there were few instances of retired agents continuing to work at the FBI. I also reasoned that the work was for the
younger generation of FBI Agents who were well equipped to deal
with the problems set before them. I also discovered that, because
of my background, a number of the seminarians and two professors
sought my counsel about this terrible event for our country. I settled
in and knew that I was where I was meant to be.

While I thought I was done with the FBI, in reality I was not.
My years as an investigator, supervisor and senior executive had so
penetrated and informed my life that it often became the background
to sermons and some of my pastoral counseling. The following sermon concretely reflects that influence.

"There is an old debate about whether the Bible can be
interpreted properly only by believers or if interpretation
is open to everyone. On the one hand, the answer is obvious. Anyone can read and interpret the Bible. It is a public
book. When it comes to deciding upon a Greek text, or
translating a phrase, or reading an historical assessment
there are no special advantages that accrue to believers.

However, the debate may point us in a different direction.
The lens through which we read and understand these stories contextually, as a believer or nonbeliever, may have a
great deal to do with the impact of the story. Only if Jesus
is alive and active beyond the confines of the story -- and
only if Jesus acts in our present lives -- can the Gospel
story be experienced as the beginning of the good news.
If Jesus is absent and God is silent to us, Mark's Gospel
-- indeed all of the Bible -- can only be experienced as

disappointing and unsettling. We have that potential in the Gospel story today.

In the first chapter of Mark we have three stories: 1) the exorcism of the demon- possessed man in Capernaum (and the news traveled fast to all parts of Galilee); 2) the healing of Peter's mother-in-law (and the crowd closes in); 3) today's reading about the healing of the leper (and the healed man disobeys Jesus and tells everyone of his good news about his cleansing or healing).

Mark created a tension in these vignettes to illustrate that Jesus did not come to settle in at Capernaum as a local healer and holy man to win the adulation of the crowds through working miracles. Thus, when the crowds press for His healing touch, Jesus withdraws to pray and teach the disciples what is to come, namely, the crucifixion. Mark's purpose in this section of Chapter One is to focus on the divine authority of Jesus to do mighty and power- ful things. Jesus is a preacher and healer, but He is much more. He is the Christ -- the Son of God.

Yet, how can we read these stories about Jesus, the exor- cist and healer, without feeling cheated? God, or Jesus, has only to will it, and a person is healed. Most of us here have prayed for some kind of healing in our lives, perhaps for ourselves or for our loved ones. In the face of termi- nal illness or some disaster, many of us have prayed for a miracle.

I said at the outset that only if Jesus is alive and active beyond the confines of the story -- and only if Jesus acts in our present lives -- can the Gospel begin to be lived as good news. How then do we experience Jesus, the healer? At an even more fundamental level, perhaps, we should ask if we believe in miracles.

I once was an FBI Agent. I worked criminal investigations and national security matters for almost 34 years, and during my years "on the street," as we called it, I investigated and arrested some of the most reprehensible people you could ever possibly imagine.

The Mafia members, slippery con artists, rapists, murderers and leather-jacketed outlaw motorcycle gang members with whom I dealt over the years were at times terrifying yet somehow fascinating, and always challenging. Some of them were so mean and evil they seemed to be beyond any possible forgiveness and redemption. Some were so lost and trapped in lives and circumstances there was little they understood or to which they felt connected, outside of their criminal ways. This was particularly true of the members of the Mafia and outlaw motorcycle gangs because those groups purported to be family -- their only true families.

In one remarkable case, I spent eighteen months, day in and day out, working with an outlaw motorcycle gang member who had gotten caught up in a drug deal and, to get himself a better jail term, he decided to cooperate with the FBI and to testify against his many enemies as well as his friends and associates. He was 33 years old at the time and had lived a violent and drug-filled life since the age of eight or nine.

During our first meetings, this tall, dark man with darting eyes was menacing and vague. He was much like a caged or trapped animal, forced to cooperate with the enemy. We verbally fenced and jousted. We did not trust one another and he hated my probing questions.

When a life-long criminal decides to cooperate with the FBI, the managing agent must debrief this person on every criminal act he or she has ever committed, participated in, or has knowledge of. It is part of the deal! Even for a hardened criminal, this is a very difficult process of "confession," for there are unspeakable things that even they do not want to reveal.

It is also very hard to hear these "confessions," because the details are often horrific and an affront to everything you have been taught or that you value. After months of holding this outlaw "biker" in protective custody and debriefing him daily, I came to know him well. He knew me well, also. He was intelligent, energetic and almost always, cheerful. I was surprised by his good humor and wit. At times, he was almost likable.

Make no mistake, he was a killer, a consummate con artist and manipulator without equal. Yet, I began to see he was much more than that. I was surprised to find that he was like me in some ways: sometimes afraid, sometimes bold. As we became more comfortable with each other in this strange dance of wits and unlikely partnership, I asked him how he could have done some of the horrible crimes he described. I was always interested in "the reason why," or the motive.

One evening after a particularly long debriefing I asked, in a rather exasperated fashion, how he could have done such terrible things. He understood my question and my tone. He somehow knew I wanted to understand him.

He said, "Perry, I know most of what I have done in my life is bad, but I liked doing it. It was fun. When I look at myself in the mirror, though, I don't say to myself, 'I am a terrible person,' or 'I did a horrible thing today.'"

His words shocked and amazed me. Our culture has a number of familiar idiomatic expressions about the power of the mirror. "I couldn't look at myself in the mirror, if I did that." "A mirror has two images." "A mirror never lies." I thought: Surely this man had to see himself as "an awful person."

Today's reading is about our lives being cleansed and changed by the presence and power of Jesus Christ. This Jesus, the miracle worker -- who quiets the raging seas, expels demons and heals leprosy -- He is the model for us. It is His life we are called to imitate and live as best we can. In today's Gospel, Jesus is a miraculous healer. We are to be the same.

While we might not think of ourselves as miracle workers, clearly, by the example of the life and works of Jesus, we should expect to see, hear and participate in miracles. How does this happen?

In his book, *Living Buddha, Living Christ*, Thich Nhat Hanh, helps to point the way. Listen to these words carefully: "Christians have to help Jesus Christ be manifested by their way of life, showing those around them that love, understanding and tolerance are possible. This will not be accomplished just by books and sermons. It has to be realized by the way we live." Live as Christ lived; that is to say, act in love and understanding and tolerance -- and God is manifest. If we do, miracles happen and we will be changed.

By now, some of you are wondering about my story of the outlaw motorcycle gang member who failed to see himself in the mirror. You see, he and I became the unlikeliest of participants in a miracle. When this outlaw biker testified for the government, a defense attorney, in a very demeaning tone, accused him of having become a friend of the FBI because of the protection we gave him and the favorable jail term he would get in exchange for his testimony.

His response surprised the entire courtroom. "I don't particularly like the FBI, but I do consider Agent Smith to be my friend because he is the first man, or really the first authority figure in my life, to include my father, who did not curse me or belittle me in some way."

Believe you me, FBI Agents and criminals do not become friends, and even if it happened to be true, one did not confess it, particularly for the court record.

You see, something had happened that I was completely unaware of -- I had begun to see this outlaw, this man who had committed despicable and horrible acts, as a human being -- not the animal I first considered him to be. And he had begun to trust, perhaps for the first time in his life.

I recall the day we secretly arranged for him to enter a plea with the court and receive his sentence. As he was brought into the courtroom by other agents, I knew something was wrong. He would not look at me as I waited with the government's attorney. When the judge asked for his plea, he said, "Not guilty!" We were stunned. The judge demanded an explanation.

He turned and pointed to me, saying, "I do not trust that agent. I am getting railroaded here!"

The judge instructed us to regroup during a 10-minute recess.

When I asked him, "What happened? What was wrong?" he said, "I'm scared. How can I believe the promises you have made? Are you sure I'm only going to get seven years?"

I found myself saying, "You have to trust me. I'm all you've got." We returned to the court and he entered his plea. As agreed by all parties, he received his seven-year prison sentence.

This motorcycle gang member and I were profoundly changed by the miracle of trust and friendship. God had been with us, even though we both were quite unaware of it.

It does matter how we read and interpret the Bible. If we are believers, then, on some level, these Bible stories, whether historical fact, allegory or myth, come to life for us or impact us because we can see them in the context of how God has acted in the lives of others. This insight gives us a sense of how God just might act in our lives. We come away knowing something about what we can expect from God.

Most of us have experienced small and large miracles whether we realize it or not. In reality, God's miracles are all around us every day. We need not feel cheated or excluded. Look beyond the mere beauty of a sunset and think of the amazing graciousness of our Creator. Look beyond the comforting words we give or receive during illness and wonder at the grace and power God gives to us in difficult times. Look into the eyes of your children and your parents at that precise and tender moment when you absolutely know that you are loved and realize God loved you first. Look for the miracles. Expect and believe Jesus to be there with you and He will be. Amen+"

16 ✠

Priest

*Those who believe they believe in God, but without pas-
sion in the heart, without anguish of mind, without uncertainty, without doubt, and even at times without despair,
believe only in the idea of God, and not God himself.*

Miguel de Unamuno y Jugo

When a priest is ordained in the Episcopal Church, the preacher of the day is responsible for giving the one to be ordained what
is known as "the charge." It comes near the end of the sermon when
the priest-to-be is asked to stand and the preacher offers the candidate a few words of wisdom about what it means to be a priest. Often
these words are a mixture of reassurance and admonishment, thus
termed the "charge." On occasion, a poignant, memorable "charge"
is given.

The one given at my ordination still rings in my ears, and has
become for me a daily reminder of how I must live out my remaining years, ever mindful that all that I am as a person, Christian and

priest, belongs to God.

Dean of the Cathedral of the Incarnation, The Very Reverend Van Gardner, said, "Perry, love the people, preach the gospel... and for God's sake, get out of the way."

His words were an amazing distillation of the Christian life and the leadership model Jesus gave us. It is a rare day I do not hear an echo of his words. Somehow, these few words, "the charge," bring perspective and balance to my life.

My ministry takes me to folks in medical crisis almost daily, where I am privileged to witness, watch and wait. Pray and cry. Die a little each time somebody dies. Rejoice in the recoveries.

These visits are never predictable or routine. It is most often in these hospital rooms, nursing homes or hospice facilities, that Gardner's words give me solace and a sense of why I am in the middle of it all. My helplessness, often manifest in not knowing exactly what to say or do, is quieted only when I remember that I am there to love that person, bring the gospel in word and by example, and get out of the way.

*****

The oxygen running through a tube connected to a regulating device on the wall keeps Gwyneth tethered... I watch and wait. She is a smart, beautiful thirty-year-old with cystic fibrosis, and by all accounts she has lived much longer than most who have this dreadful, killing disease.

I sit for hours with her since she is in crisis and death may come at any moment. Her husband, doctors, Mom and Dad, all shuttle in and out, with little to say or do since we are either at a rallying point or deathwatch.

We pray for recovery, another passing of crisis… a second chance. We are desperate for her to live; she is so precious and loved. My mind searches for something --anything to take me away from her struggle to breathe. I begin to visualize the hundreds of hospital rooms I have visited.

All hospital rooms (although not the ICU) seem to have windows. In a semi-private room, the better bed is the window bed, but it is usually taken. Options in hospitals are limited, so holding out for a private room guarantees a window, but how many can afford it? Johns Hopkins, the Washington Hospital Center, the Mayo Clinic and many other hospitals in America provide separate rooms, and in some cases, corridors or wings for America's elite – the rich and highly successful. Privilege and what money can buy are realities.

Some hospital rooms, mostly the private ones, have a place for flowers. It is no surprise that if a patient has a family and numerous friends, they get a lot of flowers. What saddens me, however, is that if a patient is a loner and has few friends, they will not get flowers, not even from their family. So, I try to bring flowers to the loners.

Some hospital personnel do not seem to like flowers because they get in the way of equipment and efficiency. There is the ubiquitous potty or urinal somewhere in plain view, and these artifacts seem to embarrass some women, especially older ones. But men don't give a damn. "Hand me the urinal, will ya?" they say. There is something incongruent about urinals being on the same tables with flowers or food. Yet, that seems to be where they are always found. I recently saw flowers beautifully arranged in an upright urinal. The patient was pretty pleased with himself for thinking of this novel use.

Hospital beds will contort into all sorts of positions, creaking and groaning as electric motors whirl and strain to find the desired position. If patients are alert and ambulatory, they are permitted to control how the bed is positioned. Finding a comfortable position in a hospital bed is nearly impossible. Nurses know this impossibility and hate trying. I suppose many doctors don't know how because I have seen several refuse to adjust a patient's bed, deferring instead to an aide or a nurse to tackle the impossible. A spouse or friend is the best person to adjust a hospital bed because they will try to get it right, no matter what.

Intravenous (IV) stands or trees are fascinating contraptions with multiple plastic bags variously filled and hung without any seeming order; all are connected into a main tube which usually terminates into a catheter stuck into the patient's arm or hand. Even though these catheters, as opposed to an 18 or 20 gauge needle, are less likely to cause a vein to "blow," it still hurts like hell getting stuck. As I watch a nurse or technician search for the perfect vein, and probe with the needle for placement, I wince and squirm right along with the patient. Nurses or technicians who can "stick" a vein and get a good flow on the first try are worth their weight in gold.

On a modern IV tree there is a box that beeps when something is out of sync. They must be frequently unsynchronized because the beeping box never seems to stop making its noise. When this happens a nurse will run into the room, look at the box seriously, furiously punch in six to nine numbers (never fewer than six), look at the bags, then the box again, pronounce, "Everything is fine," and then rush out of the room.

A good nurse will tell the patient what happened. Most don't explain much these days because they are too busy doing paperwork. The better nurses hate paperwork and would rather be caring for their patients.

Hospital smells keep some away from visiting friends and family. Most hospitals do a pretty good job of keeping their spaces clean, but scuff marks, blood and trash all over a room can, and usually do, speak of the serious measures taken to help or save someone. The patient's loved ones will be upset by this mess if they sense what has gone on.

The smell of death, however, has nothing to do with the room or the tidiness of a place. It is the patient's body letting off gases and other odors that have a particular and peculiar smell that experienced hospital visitors know immediately. When the less experienced visitor is told… really told…what the smell means, those in the room become quiet and the deathwatch begins.

It seems to me that spiritual people know when death is imminent, often long before the obvious occurs. It may be because they have a gift of discernment. This gift heightens the senses and makes these people keenly aware of things others might miss.

Country folk, for some reason, are quick to know when death approaches, and they signal the watch by whispered speech and respectful concern for the family members who will usually grieve mightily. Witnessing these sacred times during my childhood when my grandparents and other relatives died, I know these folks are often spiritual and compassionate. Their prayers become more fervent because they know that a Holy death is a good death.

Suffering is the enemy and they pray hard that any suffering ends quickly. These folk will never use rude language to explain. They will gently say things like, "Daddy's going home," or "Mommy's going to a better place," or "She's going to the Lord."

Mercifully, most survive hospital stays. Some die. Death is the ultimate insult for medical professionals. Dying is hard business. Yet, there are times when we want to die. Loneliness and isolation kill more of us than we are willing to admit. Dying instantly from an aneurysm or a shot to the head is far easier than dying inch-by-inch from ALS or a slow malicious cancer or just plain old age.

*****

I continue to watch and wait on the God I trust, and on the Gwyneth who loves life and wants to live. I ponder what it is to be a prisoner in a hospital room. Most of us, at one point or another, are likely to pass through a hospital. "It is better to be a visitor," I mused.

Three weeks passed and Gwyneth rallied. Chatting about this recent episode, we were interrupted by the senior physician on Gwyneth's pulmonary care team. Noticing my priest collar, the doctor asked that I leave, but Gwyneth told her I would stay. Her parents and husband were at their jobs that afternoon.

The doctor began, "Gwyneth, I am here to apologize to you for the errors that were made in the precipitous shutting down of your chest vacuum, putting you into crisis. It was a mistake that should have never happened, and I am responsible. I am sorry."

I was astounded by her honesty and clarity.

"You nearly killed me," Gwyneth exploded, "And that is all you can say!"

The doctor calmly continued, "It was a case of too many cooks in the kitchen. The surgeon did not understand that your chest vacuum had to remain on for a longer period of time, regardless of the good lung function and inflation at the time he saw you. He shut off the vacuum and ordered the removal of your chest tube. However, by the time the nurse realized what he had done, you were in crisis. I promise nothing like this will ever happen again. No orders will be executed without my specific approval from here on."

"If I survive long enough to leave this hospital, I will never come back here," Gwyneth spewed. "I will find another hospital, other doctors, who know what they are doing. You nearly killed me with a simple flip of a switch! Damn it! How can I trust you with anything more complicated?"

The doctor took the assault, impressing me, but Gwyneth was determined, angry beyond measure, and turning to me she said, "Perry, you have got to get me out of here before they kill me."

Now just a bit embarrassed for both the doctor and Gwyneth, I nodded affirmatively. The doctor realized there was nothing to placate Gwyneth now, so she left the room.

Several days passed and Gwyneth was discharged to begin the search for another hospital and surgical team with a highly successful lung transplant program. It was her only hope and option. Her lungs were completely compromised, and the disease would continue to scar her alveoli and mangle her ability to breathe. She had to get on a new transplant list quickly; time was running out.

*****

Gwyneth's health continued to deteriorate. After some months of driving more than sixty miles between Fairfax, Virginia, and Baltimore, Maryland, for assessments and treatments, she was finally put on the lung transplant list at Inova Fairfax Hospital. This was good news because their success rate with transplants was considerably higher than most other hospitals in the region. Still, there was more waiting and a couple of false alarms as opportunities for tissue matches failed. Our spirits were lifted when Gwyneth was put near the top of the transplant eligibility list.

My time at Emmanuel Church, Baltimore, came to an end and Gwyneth honored me by being present at my farewell celebration of ministry even though she was in severe pulmonary distress. During my remarks I mentioned three people who had taught me a great deal about faithfulness and devotion, especially Gwyneth for her courage in the face of her terminal illness and her amazing resolve to go on living as long as she could and as best she could. It was an emotional, heartfelt, tearful event. My next parish was to be in St. Augustine, Florida, a very long distance away.

Gwyneth and I stayed in frequent contact by telephone and I visited her on occasion when I was in the Baltimore-Washington area. As luck would have it, I was in Northern Virginia visiting my daughters, when Gwyneth finally received her call for a probable transplant. Her father called to tell me the news and asked me to meet them at the hospital. I arrived at about 4 p.m. to find Gwyneth, her husband and her mother and father waiting for the surgeon's arrival to discuss whether or not there was a tissue match.

The doctor came in soon thereafter and announced, "The lungs are perfect for you, Gwyneth, and all that is left is for you to say yes." We all were silent for a few moments, letting this long-awaited news sink in, and the doctor then said, "Gwyneth, you have a 50-50 chance of surviving this surgery tonight, and you must understand that before giving me your answer."

Gwyneth scanned our waiting faces and replied, "Absolutely. Let's go. Without this surgery I will surely die."

She knew the odds, she also knew that even with new lungs, she might get only another three to five years of life, but it was worth the risk. We all nodded in agreement. The doctor said she would be moved to a pre-op suite in the surgery area in a short while. We all prayed together and then the doctor hurried from the room. Gwyneth's family and I were soon trailing her down the hallway as she was pushed along on a stretcher. Once in the pre-op area, IVs were started and interrogatories by a nurse and the anesthesiologist followed.

There was a pall of fear and seriousness in the room broken by what turned out to be a question that lightened our mood a bit. As the nurse proceeded through her questionnaire, she asked Gwyneth, "Do you have any exotic piercings that we need to know about?"

And before Gwyneth answered, her mother asked, "What in the world does that mean?" Gwyneth smiled, looked at me, and said, "Perry, will you tell Mother later what that means?" Smiling back, I nodded in agreement. She then told the nurse that she had no exotic piercings.

It was not long before Gwyneth was moved into the operating room, leaving us behind to our private thoughts and prayers. The surgery would last all night and so we retired to the waiting room, fortified with coffee and something to eat from the hospital cafeteria. As we waited I did explain exotic piercings to Gwyneth's mother, but I'm not sure she ever completely understood how or why any woman might do such a thing. Evening turned into night, and the night into dawn, and the new day brought a celebration of renewed hope for Gwyneth.

The double-lung transplant was successful and gave Gwyneth an additional three years of life. During those years, she and her husband, joined by family and friends, took hiking trips to Scotland, Mount St. Helens, Yellowstone National Park and the Olympic peninsula in Washington State. All of this outdoor activity reflected Gwyneth's long term love for the environmental sciences and her profession as a hydro-geologist. Whether she had three or five years or ten minutes of life left, Gwyneth filled the time with these joyous outings and living life to the fullest.

Gwyneth, who despite being diagnosed with cystic fibrosis when she was 18 months old, became a successful athlete and out-doorswoman while working as a hydro-geologist, and lived well beyond even the most optimistic expectations for someone with cystic fibrosis. Cystic fibrosis is always terminal and is caused by a defective gene that causes the body to create large amounts of mu-cus leading to lung infections, digestive disorders and other health problems. The respiratory distress that Gwyneth suffered in the later years of her life was unbelievably painful and wrenching, and be-ing tethered to an oxygen bottle frustrated Gwyneth, but she never complained. She thought of it as something like the hurdles she ran in track during high school and college, one more thing that had to be dealt with.

As if the cystic fibrosis was not enough, two years after the transplant, Gwyneth was diagnosed with acute myelogenous leuke-mia, a fast-growing cancer of the blood and bone marrow, and she began chemotherapy treatments. After seven months of treatment, she relapsed and her situation became desperate. E-mails asking for prayers circulated among her many friends and family. More treatments followed, but to no avail. Her father telephoned on April 29, 2008, to tell me that Gwyneth had died of respiratory failure.

Emmanuel Episcopal Church was filled with family and friends, and the remembrances and stories told that day were vintage dry Scottish humor and melancholia drenched in tears and laughter. Gwyneth, like the good Scots woman she so proudly was, had more courage, stamina and grace about her illness and her life, than I had ever seen in a person. She lived life on her own terms, without complaint or regret, and I was honored to be her friend and priest.

It is into this sacred, intimate space… birth, new life, death and dying… that a priest enters. Birth is celebrated in baptism, marking the child as Christ's own forever. The sacrament of marriage inaugurates and blesses a new life together in hope of becoming as one. Burial celebrates the life of a soul departed this earthly existence: the sending off, called into that eternal, heavenly place where there is no suffering or pain. To my mind, there is no greater privilege than to be invited into these sacred or "thin times," as the Irish would call them.

*****

Alan Jones, in his book, *Sacrifice and Delight*, touches a deep cord somewhere inside me when he says, "The Church needs lovers. The Church needs those who know the secret of self-offering, the secret of sacrifice and delight." This is the language that communicates the passion and desire I have for being at the altar… in praise, thanksgiving, celebration and sacrifice… and never wanting it to end. It is the lover in me that is excited, energized and full of expectation when I preach or celebrate the Eucharist, always wanting to touch the hearers in a way that brings Jesus into their lives in a relevant and real way.

I know that God's claim on my life is absolute and I so desire to see His face; to know His presence; to have His mercy; and to experience Him in the Incarnate Christ. He is the mystery to be sought, yet He is the pursuer. He is elusive, yet constant. For some existential reason, the crucifixion brings Jesus' humanity and divinity into sharp focus and reality for me. The Jesus I know best is the sufferer, the crucified One, redeemer and savior.

My sense and experience of the crucified Christ began at a very early age, perhaps seven, eight or nine, when I became acutely aware of and drawn to the crucifixes on the rosaries hanging from the belts and knotted cords of the nuns who taught us catechism. I was struck by the stark dominance, and strange beauty of the crucifix, no matter how big or small, in the rooms and halls of our homes, classrooms and churches. I also felt a persistent, strong yearning to be at God's altar. I served as an altar boy as soon as I could because it put me closer to God's "place and home (the tabernacle)."

Part of the reason I experience God through the crucified Christ was that I understood, without really knowing why, that His death was a mystery, a sacred mystery, and I wanted to know the secret and become part of it. I also had a sense that Jesus was alone in His death, save perhaps His Mother and the beloved disciple. I have felt very alone during many periods of my life, and by being in His presence, hung on the cross, I was not alone; nor was He.

I started praying the Daily Office in my early teens and out of that discipline, I came to love the psalms and the rhythm, continuity and stability the Office gave me. In my difficulties and searching, I

knew God was with me. It was as much a part of my reason for going to the monastery as was my fascination with Thomas Merton.
In the monastery I was connected to the ancient, and through the
rhythm and discipline of prayer, I experienced the mystery of coming into the presence of the Holy.

The Trappist monastic life, even though I was only there a short
time, has shaped me and left an indelible mark on my spirituality,
theology and Christology. At the center are Jesus, crucified, and His
suffering mother, Mary… *O clemens, O pia, O dulcis Virgo Maria…*
at the foot of His cross. I, too, am there. I am persuaded that this formation in part, by God's grace, is what has made me a priest.

When I think about how I became a priest, it is now obvious
to me as well as to many of my friends that the whole of my life
has been preparation for the priesthood. Jules Pfeiffer, the renowned
cartoonist, famously told Charlie Rose in an interview about his
late-life memoir that he had not previously written a memoir because he thought it was unnecessary. He commented that, since he
knew the story, he thought it was a frivolous notion to do a memoir.
The irony, he said, was that, as he wrote the memoir, he discovered
he did not know his own story.

It is true for me as well. It is as though God had been my constant companion whether I realized it or not and somehow brought
me to this life as a priest. During all of the times I felt alone or
abandoned, in truth I never was. This writing has raised from my
memory all those people who helped, encouraged and supported me
through difficult times. In retrospect, it seems that each and every
one of them came into my life at critical times and, without overdra-
matizing, basically saved my life or gave me a new opportunity to

move forward.

Most of my ordained life as a deacon and a priest has been focused on the poor, the disenfranchised and those marginalized by loneliness, isolation and illness. Another priest's wife once described me as "a priest to those who have fallen through the cracks." Others have described me as being "real, not the holier-than-thou type." I think both characterizations fit. It is with some pride, I suppose, that I want always to be "real" because I am first a man, and in becoming a priest, I did not check my humanity at the door. It has been my observation that some religious people tend to forget that Jesus was fully human as well as divine, but that it was principally His humanity that set the example for others and brought the people to Him.

The life of a priest, in my view, is not much different from that of a layperson at its root. We all are commanded to love God with our hearts, souls and minds and our neighbors as ourselves; it is simply that the path is different. A priest must focus on our real world, but we also must live much of life in the mystical world. It is not easy and few choose this life. Nonetheless, it is in the mystical world that the Holy Spirit lives, enlivening and enabling us to live a Christian life.

My favorite theologian, Frederick Buechner, has said that it is not the object of life to make prayer but rather to live life in prayer. It is there that we find God and His Holy Spirit. It is the work of the priest to pray and to encourage others to do the same.

The ultimate prayer for me is Holy Eucharist. It is at the moment of what is known as the fraction when the priest breaks the bread and says, "Alleluia. Christ, our Passover, is sacrificed for us," that the real and mystical worlds converge… the alpha and omega of our existence comes together. It is here that I find the deepest meaning and joy of my priesthood. It is here that I feel whole and complete…at one with God and my neighbors.

Ordination to the priesthood, May 25, 2002,
Cathedral of the Incarnation, Baltimore

One more time at age 63, Tlaxcala, Mexico.

About the author

The Rev. J. Perry Smith is an Episcopal priest who presently serves as the
Canon for Pastoral Care at St. John's
Cathedral in Jacksonville, Florida. This
is his first book. He his currently writing *Adoption Matters...* personal stories from adoptees and parents on both
sides of the adoption. Fr. Smith and his
wife Lisa reside in Jacksonville, Flori-
da. Together they have three daughters, Amy, Meghan and Krista, and two
grandchildren, Briana and Graer.

Visit his web site at: jperrysmithbooks.com or contact him at info@
jperrysmithbooks.com.

CPSIA information can be obtained at www.ICGtesting.com
Printed in the USA
LVOW061549031111

253399LV00006B/43/P

9 780983 966906